Learning Robotic Process Automation

Automation

Create Software robots and automate business processes
with the leading RPA tool – UiPath

Alok Mani Tripathi

BIRMINGHAM - MUMBAI

Learning Robotic Process Automation

Copyright © 2018 Packt Publishing

Commissioning Editor: Kunal Chaudhari
Acquisition Editor: Noyonika Das
Content Development Editor: Roshan Kumar
Technical Editor: Harshal Kadam
Copy Editor: Safis Editing
Project Coordinator: Hardik Bhinde
Proofreader: Safis Editing
Indexer: Mariammal Chettiyar
Graphics: Jason Monteiro
Production Coordinator: Nilesh Mohite

First published: March 2018

Production reference: 1270318

Published by Packt Publishing Ltd.
Livery Place
35 Livery Street
Birmingham
B3 2PB, UK.

ISBN 978-1-78847-094-0

www.packtpub.com

mapt.io

Mapt is an online digital library that gives you full access to over 5,000 books and videos, as well as industry leading tools to help you plan your personal development and advance your career. For more information, please visit our website.

Why subscribe?

- Spend less time learning and more time coding with practical eBooks and Videos from over 4,000 industry professionals

- Improve your learning with Skill Plans built especially for you

- Get a free eBook or video every month

- Mapt is fully searchable

- Copy and paste, print, and bookmark content

PacktPub.com

Did you know that Packt offers eBook versions of every book published, with PDF and ePub files available? You can upgrade to the eBook version at www.PacktPub.com and as a print book customer, you are entitled to a discount on the eBook copy. Get in touch with us at service@packtpub.com for more details.

At www.PacktPub.com, you can also read a collection of free technical articles, sign up for a range of free newsletters, and receive exclusive discounts and offers on Packt books and eBooks.

Contributors

About the author

Alok Mani Tripathi is the founder of RPATech (RPATech.in), which is a leading end-to-end consulting and services company with a focus on RPA and AI. He is an early adopter of RPA and has been connected with various RPA tools providers and analysts. He has trained 200+ people on different RPA platforms. Alok has created and led multiple RPA **Center of Excellence (CoE)** for global organizations with a clear focus on cognitive and service delivery automation. He is a long-time contributor to the RPA community and maintains a community group with a huge following on LinkedIn.

About the reviewer

Saibal Goswami has a career spanning more than 12 years, in which he has developed a strong competency in partnership management, client relationships, project management, business analysis, and operations management. He cultivated these competencies through an efficient process feasibility study, cost/benefit analyses, resource planning, and leading and mentoring cross-functional teams in order to maximize productivity. Saibal has been associated with RPA since the beginning. He has mastered various technical skills, such as RPA process assessment and RPA CoE, among others.

Packt is searching for authors like you

If you're interested in becoming an author for Packt, please visit authors.packtpub.com and apply today. We have worked with thousands of developers and tech professionals, just like you, to help them share their insight with the global tech community. You can make a general application, apply for a specific hot topic that we are recruiting an author for, or submit your own idea.

Table of Contents

Preface

In today's digital world, enterprises are looking toward cost-efficient digital delivery. **Robotics Process Automation (RPA)** is a rapidly growing technology that helps enterprises automate processes by mimicking human action on computers, thereby delivering faster with consistent quality. Many cognitive abilities are now being introduced in this technology. UiPath is a leading RPA platform and is the fastest way of automating business processes. This book will take you on a journey where you will come to understand RPA technology and get your hands dirty in building bots to automate processes. This book will enable you to become ready for the future of RPA.

Who this book is for

This book is for anyone who wants to get started with their career in RPA. Basic knowledge of C#/ VB.NET is required.

What this book covers

Chapter 1, *What is Robotic Process Automation?*, In this chapter, readers will get to know about the history of automation and the advent of RPA. What types of automation can be categorized as RPA? What do future analysts predict? Who are the major players in the market? What are the benefits of RPA? All this is covered in this chapter.

Chapter 2, *Record and Play*, In this chapter, readers will be introduced to UiPath Stack and Process Designer/Studio, and will use wizard-based tools to quickly automate mundane tasks.

Chapter 3, *Sequence, Flowchart, Control Flow*, examines the project that was generated by the recorder and get an explain the program flow (Workflow). Readers will also understand the use of sequences and the nesting of activities. Readers will learn to use the building blocks of a Workflow Flowchart and Control flow (for looping and decision making).

Chapter 4, *Data Manipulation*, teaches techniques to use memory with variables. Readers will also learn about data tables to store data in and easy ways to manipulate data in memory. This chapter also shows how disk files (CSV, Excel, and so on) are used to persist data.

Chapter 5, *Take Control of the Controls*, states that extraction is a primary feature of RPA which enables UI automation. Behind the scenes, many technologies are at work to seamless extract information from the UI. When typical RPA techniques are not successful, OCR technology is used to extract information. In this chapter, readers will learn about various *selectors* available in UiPath to extract and take action on controls. We will use one browser-based application to accomplish the task explained in each section. In the end, we will automate one Windows application task.

Chapter 6, *Tame that Application with Plugins and Extensions*, UiPath has many plugins and extensions to simplify UI automation. Apart from basic extraction and interaction with the desktop screen, these plugins allow users to directly interact with that application or simplify UI automation. Readers will learn about the use of these plugins and extensions. Each section has examples and use cases.

Chapter 7, *Handling User Events and Assistant Bots*, in this chapter, readers will learn about Assistant bot its utility. All monitoring events that can be used to trigger actions have been covered, and two examples of monitoring events have also been given.

Chapter 8, *Exception Handling, Debugging, and Logging*, in this chapter, readers will learn to use exception handling techniques, log errors screenshots, and find out other useful information to be used for debugging or reporting. Readers will learn how to debug code.

Chapter 9, *Managing and* Maintaining *the Code*, covers the organization of the project, modularity techniques, workflow nesting, and using a TFS server to maintain versions of the source code.

Chapter 10, *Deploying and Maintaining the Bot*, in this chapter, readers will learn about publishing utility and Orchestration server. Readers will also learn how a production environment is prepared.

To get the most out of this book

A basic understanding of C#/ VB.NET, a laptop to work on an, installation of UiPath Studio, and this book is all you need to get started with your bot making process!

Download the example code files

You can download the example code files for this book from your account at www.packtpub.com. If you purchased this book elsewhere, you can visit www.packtpub.com/support and register to have the files emailed directly to you.

You can download the code files by following these steps:

1. Log in or register at www.packtpub.com.
2. Select the **SUPPORT** tab.
3. Click on **Code Downloads & Errata**.
4. Enter the name of the book in the **Search** box and follow the onscreen instructions.

Once the file is downloaded, please make sure that you unzip or extract the folder using the latest version of:

- WinRAR/7-Zip for Windows
- Zipeg/iZip/UnRarX for Mac
- 7-Zip/PeaZip for Linux

The code bundle for the book is also hosted on GitHub at https://github.com/PacktPublishing/Learning-Robotic-Process-Automation. We also have other code bundles from our rich catalog of books and videos available at https://github.com/PacktPublishing/. Check them out!

Download the color images

We also provide a PDF file that has color images of the screenshots/diagrams used in this book. You can download it here: https://www.packtpub.com/sites/default/files/downloads/LearningRoboticProcessAutomation_ColorImages.pdf.

Conventions used

There are a number of text conventions used throughout this book.

CodeInText: Indicates code words in text, database table names, folder names, filenames, file extensions, pathnames, dummy URLs, user input, and Twitter handles. Here is an example: "In our case, we have put in "What's your name?"."

Bold: Indicates a new term, an important word, or words that you see onscreen. For example, words in menus or dialog boxes appear in the text like this. Here is an example: "Add an **Input dialog** activity inside the **Sequence**."

 Warnings or important notes appear like this.

 Tips and tricks appear like this.

Get in touch

Feedback from our readers is always welcome.

General feedback: Email `feedback@packtpub.com` and mention the book title in the subject of your message. If you have questions about any aspect of this book, please email us at `questions@packtpub.com`.

Errata: Although we have taken every care to ensure the accuracy of our content, mistakes do happen. If you have found a mistake in this book, we would be grateful if you would report this to us. Please visit `www.packtpub.com/submit-errata`, selecting your book, clicking on the Errata Submission Form link, and entering the details.

Piracy: If you come across any illegal copies of our works in any form on the Internet, we would be grateful if you would provide us with the location address or website name. Please contact us at `copyright@packtpub.com` with a link to the material.

If you are interested in becoming an author: If there is a topic that you have expertise in and you are interested in either writing or contributing to a book, please visit `authors.packtpub.com`.

Reviews

Please leave a review. Once you have read and used this book, why not leave a review on the site that you purchased it from? Potential readers can then see and use your unbiased opinion to make purchase decisions, we at Packt can understand what you think about our products, and our authors can see your feedback on their book. Thank you!

For more information about Packt, please visit packtpub.com.

1
What is Robotic Process Automation?

Nowadays, there is almost no aspect of our lives that is unaffected by automation. Some examples include washing machines, microwave ovens, autopilot mode for automobiles and airplanes, Nestlé using Robots to sell coffee pods in stores in Japan, Walmart testing drones to deliver products in the US, our bank checks being sorted using **Optical Character Recognition (OCR)**, and ATMs.

The term automation is derived from the Greek words *autos* meaning self, and *motos*, meaning moving. It is believed to have been coined in the 1940s when there was an increased use of automated devices in mechanized production lines in the Ford Motor Company.

Automation, in simple words, is technology that deals with the application of machines and computers to the production of goods and services. This helps in getting work done with little or no human assistance.

With the advent of computers, many software systems were developed to accomplish tasks that were previously done on paper to manage businesses, or not being done at all due to the lack of tools. Some of these are bookkeeping, inventory management, and communications management.

There is also a type of software that ties these systems and people together in workflows, known as **Business Process Management (BPM)** tools. This software has been developed for areas such as record systems, engagement systems, insight systems, and innovation systems. These mostly replicate processes in real-life scenarios.

In the digital world, automation and software development are two different terms. Very often, however, one is confused with the other. If some portion of a workflow can be programmed to be done without human intervention, it can be called automation. For example, in order to pass any invoice in a payment system, Ms. Julia at ABC organization needs to check that goods have been delivered and recorded in an inventory management system. This is a cumbersome job, as it has to be done for each and every invoice. Also, for larger organizations, more people are needed to do this check on computers. However, Jack, an application developer, proposes that he can integrate those two systems using database integration techniques. He will write a procedure that will fetch data from the inventory management system and automate the check of receivables.

Developing an inventory management software system is called software development, while programming a step so that no more human intervention is required is called automation.

In this chapter, you will learn about the basic concepts of automation and Robotic process automation.

Scope and techniques of automation

There are various techniques used and available to automate steps and processes in an organization where software systems are being used to accomplish certain tasks. Before we look at these techniques however, let us see what *can* be automated and what *should* be automated.

What should be automated?

There are a few aspects that have to be taken into consideration for choosing automation candidates. The following processes should be automated:

- Repetitive steps
- Time-consuming steps
- High-risk tasks
- Tasks with a low-quality yield
- Tasks involving multiple people and multiple steps
- And everything else!

We have found out what should be automated. Now the question arises what *can* be automated?

What can be automated?

In order to automate something, it needs to have the following characteristics:

- Well defined and rule-based steps
- Logical
- An input to the task can be diverted to the software system
- Input can be deciphered by software systems with available techniques
- The output system is accessible
- Benefits are more than the cost

Techniques of automation

There are various techniques available for automation and programmers have been using them for years to increase efficiency in enterprises:

- **Custom software**: Developing new software to perform repetitive tasks.
- **Runbook**: Runbooks are typically used for IT-based operations. They are a compilation of a set of commands or tasks that are performed for maintenance and other types of activities. Runbooks can be offline as well, often referred to as run commands for performing sets of tasks.
- **Batch**: Batch files used to very popular. They used to compile a sequence of commands that could be run by a single click or command. They can also be scheduled to be run at a specific time using the scheduler.
- **Wrapper**: Wraps around existing software or hosts client applications. The wrapper monitors activities in a client app and performs actions based on rules.

  For example:

  - Putting validation on top of a mainframe application using hummingbird
  - Hosting a website inside a shell, navigation, and actions

- **Browser automation**: Greasemonkey and many other web macro software helped in browser-based automation. It can be used to read from a website and save to a database. It can also write to fields based on rules. Using this technique, a whole website can be changed, and components can be added or removed from the website. Sometimes, it is also referred to as web scripting or web injections.

- **Desktop automation**: Traditionally, desktop automation used to mean that multiple screens on a desktop were woven together to present a single screen, and if there was some data transfer from one screen to another, it could be done automatically. Recently, assisted Robotics process automation has also been considered for desktop automation by some companies.

- **Database/web service integration**: In database integration, we read/write to a client database directly. In web service integration, we communicate with the client system using a web service:

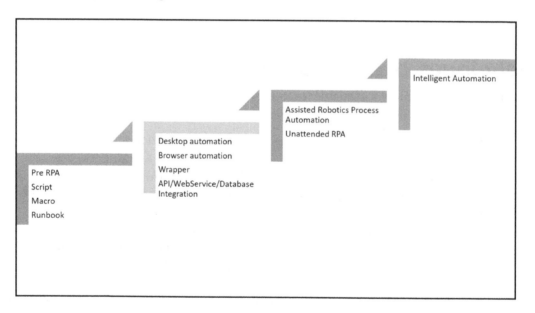

Robotic process automation

Today, automation has reached a stage of maturity where a number of other technologies have developed from it. **Robotic process automation (RPA)** is one such transformational burgeoning area. *Robot* in Robotic process automation means software programs that mimic human actions.

In simple words, RPA involves the use of software that *mimics* human actions while interacting with applications in a computer and accomplishing *rule-based tasks*. This often requires reading from and typing, or clicking on existing applications that are used to perform the given tasks.

In addition, these software Robots also perform complex calculations and decision making on the basis of the data and predefined rules. With the rapid progress of technology and renewed efforts in the area of artificial intelligence, it has become possible to use **State** activity: Transitions contain three sections—**Trigger**, **Condition**, and **Action**, which enable you to add a trigger for the next state or a condition under which an activity is to be executed. with RPA to accomplish tasks that were not possible earlier. Some of the technologies being adopted with RPA are as follows:

- Machine learning
- Natural language processing
- Natural language generation
- Computer vision

With the inclusion of the preceding technologies, sometimes it is also referred to as intelligent automation.

With the advent of RPA, it has become much easier to automate tasks. Now, we need to know only the steps taken by humans and make the Robots mimic the action on a computer screen using mouse and keyboard. This is a big deal because in most cases, the process is already defined and the steps documented. Humans also follow the same operating procedures, which define the steps taken to accomplish the task. Business logic, validation of data, transformation, and use of data is already coded in existing systems that humans use to accomplish a task, a simple example being invoice data entry.

RPA platforms allow the program, called Robots, to interact with any application in the same way a human would do, hence, automating rule-based work by recording those steps for later playback.

An important point that distinguishes RPA from traditional automation is that the software Robot is *trained* using steps that are illustrative rather than using instructions based on code. Thus, a person with little programming experience can be trained on these platforms to automate simple to complex processes.

Also, RPA software, unlike traditional automation, is capable of adapting to dynamic circumstances, for example, when checking an electronic form of new employees in a company. If the pin code is missing in a form, in traditional automation the software would point out the blank field as an exception, and then a human being would search for the relevant pin code and correct the form. In RPA however, the software is capable of performing all the BPO tasks mentioned previously with no human assistance.

From tedious, repetitive, and high volume tasks, to diverse, complicated systems that need to work together lucidly, RPA can handle it all. There is consistency in quality, accuracy, productivity and efficiency, faster delivery of services, and of course, lower operation costs.

With the constant development and integration of RPA with industries, people previously engaged in mundane, repetitive tasks can now move on to engaging themselves in higher value, better quality activities, leaving the tedious tasks to the software Robots.

What can RPA do?

Today, RPA has matured beyond doing mundane repetitive tasks, and is seen as a transformational technology that can bring tremendous value to the organization adopting it. The ability to create full audit trails is significant for improving the quality of work being done and eliminating human error. Once trained, these Robots will perform tasks with the same precision over and over again. These Robots can interact with applications irrespective of the technologies on which the applications are built. They can work with popular ERP applications such as SAP, Oracle, or Microsoft Dynamics, and BPMs such as Pega systems and Appian.

Custom applications built on .NET, Java, the command-line, or mainframe terminal are easy to use with RPA.

With the inclusion of AI technologies, RPA now has the capability to read from images or scanned documents, and it can interpret unstructured data and formats as well. However, most of the implementation is happening with structured and digital data.

Benefits of RPA

Today, RPA is being widely accepted across industries and across the world. The following industries can benefit a lot from RPA:

- **Business process outsourcing (BPO)**: With RPA and its benefits of reduced costs, the BPO sector can now depend less on outsourced labor.

- **Insurance**: The complexity and number of tasks that must be managed in the insurance sector, from managing policies, to filing and processing claims across multiple platforms, provides an ideal environment for the use of RPA technology.
- **Financial sector**: From day-to-day activities and handling an enormous amount of data, to performing complex workflows, RPA has been helping to transform this sector into an efficient and reliable one.
- **Utility companies**: These companies (such as gas, electricity, and water) deal with a lot of monetary transactions and can leverage RPA to automate tasks such as meter reading, billing, and processing customer payments.
- **Healthcare:** Data entry, patient scheduling, and more importantly billing and claims processing, are important areas where RPA can be used. RPA will help in optimizing patient appointments, sending them automatic reminders of their appointments and eliminating human error in patient records. This leaves workers to focus more on the needs of the patients, and also leads to improved patient experience.

The following are the benefits of RPA:

- **Higher quality services, greater accuracy**: With reduced human error and greater compliance, the quality of work is much better. Also, while it is difficult to trace the point at which the human error occurred, the detection of errors is much simpler in RPA. This is because every step in the automation process is recorded, making it faster to pinpoint errors with ease. A reduction, or removal of, errors also means greater accuracy of data, leading to better quality analytics and hence better decision making.

- **Improved analytics**: Since these software Robots can log each action taken with the appropriate tag and metadata, it is very easy to get business insights and other analytical data. Using analytics on the collected data such as transaction received time, transaction complete time, and predictions can be made for the incoming volume and ability to complete the tasks on time.

- **Reduced costs**: Nowadays, it is commonplace to hear that one Robot is equivalent to three human **full-time executives (FTE)**. This is based on the simple fact that one FTE works for eight hours a day, while a Robot can work for 24 hours without a break. Increased availability and productivity means the cost of operations is reduced tremendously. The speed of the work being performed coupled with multitasking results in further reductions in cost.

- **Increased speed**: Robots are very fast and sometimes the speed of execution has to be reduced to match the speed and latency of the application on which these Robots work. Increased speed can result in better response times and an increase in the volume of the tasks being performed.

- **Greater compliance**: As mentioned earlier, a full audit trail is one of the highlights of RPA and can result in greater compliance. These Robots do not deviate from the defined set of steps to be taken while doing a task and hence it will certainly result in better compliance..

- **Agility**: Reducing and increasing the number of Robot resources requires managing the volume of the business process. This is just a click away. More Robots can be deployed to perform the same task easily. Redeployment of resources does not require any kind of coding or reconfiguration.

- **Comprehensive insights**: In addition to the audit trail and time stamping, Robots can tag transactions to use them later, in reports for business insight. By using these business insights, better decisions can be made for the improvement of the business. This recorded data can also be used for forecasting.

- **Versatility**: RPA is applicable across industries performing a wide range of tasks—from small to large businesses, simple to complex processes.

- **Simplicity**: RPA does not need prior programming knowledge. Most platforms provide designs in the form of flowcharts. This simplicity enables easy automation of business processes, leaving the IT professionals relatively free to carry out higher value work. Also, since automation is carried out by people from within the department or area of work, no requirements are lost in translation between the business unit and the development team, which may have happened otherwise in traditional automation.

- **Scalability**: RPA is highly scalable, up as well as down. Whether one requires an increase or reduction in the virtual workforce, Robots can be quickly deployed at zero or minimum costs while maintaining consistency in the quality of work.

- **Time savings**: Not only does the virtual workforce complete large volumes of work in a shorter span of time with precision, but they help save time in another way too. If there is any change—say, a technology upgrade it is much easier and faster for the virtual workforce to adapt to the changes. This can be done by bringing about modifications in the programming or introducing new processes. For humans, it is difficult for them to learn and get trained in something new—breaking from the old habit of performing repetitive tasks.

- **Non- invasive**: RPA, as we know, works at the user interface just like a human would. This ensures that it can be implemented without bringing changes to the existing computer systems. This helps in reducing risks and complexities that would arise in the case of traditional IT deployments.

- **Better management**: RPA allows for managing, deploying, and monitoring Robots through a centralized platform. This also lessens the need for governance.

- **Better customer service**: Since Robots can work around the clock, capacity increases. This leaves humans to focus on customer service and satisfaction. Also, better quality of services delivered to customers at faster speeds greatly boosts customer satisfaction.

- **Increased employee satisfaction**: With repetitive, dreary tasks now being taken over by the virtual workforce, employees are not just relieved of their workload, but can also engage in better quality work that requires the use of human capabilities and strengths such as emotional intelligence, reasoning, or tending to customers. Thus, RPA doesn't take away work, it just frees humans from tedious, mind-numbing work, giving us an opportunity to engage in much more satisfying jobs.

The applicability of RPA is across industries such as banking and financial services, insurance, healthcare, manufacturing, telecom, travel, and logistics. There is also penetration in industries such as consumer products, food and beverages, and entertainment.

There are horizontals irrespective of industries' domain that have seen a higher adoption, such as in finance and accounting, human resources, and procurement.

Most successful implementations are observed in what is being called *industry-specific processes* or *domain-specific processes*, for example, *claims processing* in the insurance industry.

Components of RPA

Any Robotics process automation platform provides some basic components, which together build the platform.

The following are the basic or core components of RPA:

- **Recorder**
- **Development Studio**
- **Plugin/Extension**
- **Bot Runner**
- **Control Center**:

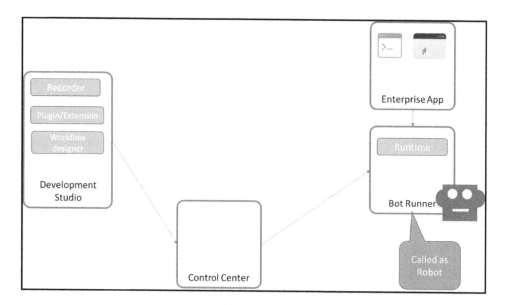

Recorder

The recorder is the part of the development studio that developers use to configure the Robots. It is like the macro recorder in Excel, the bot recorder in any platform, records steps. It records mouse and keyboard movements on the UI and this recording can be replayed to do the same steps again and again. This enables rapid automation. This component has played a very big role in the popularity of RPA. We will see the application and usefulness of this component in chapter 2, *Record and Play.*

Development studio

The development studio is used by developers to create Robot configuration or train the Robots. Using the development studio, a set of instructions and decision-making logic is coded for Robots to execute. Some platforms provide flow-charting capabilities such as Visio, so it becomes very easy to plot steps in a process, whereas some other platforms require coding. In most studios, in order to do commercial development, developers need to have a fair amount of knowledge of programming, for example, loops, if else, variable assignment, and so on. We will study the UiPath Development Studio in detail in Chapter 2, *Record and Play*.

Extensions and plugins

Most platforms offer many plugins and extensions to ease the development and running of bots. In many applications, such as Java SAP, it is not easy to individually identify controls of the UI through traditional techniques. RPA vendors have developed plugins and extensions to help with these issues. We will get to understand importance of plugins and extensions of the UiPath platform later in the book.

Bot runner

This is also referred to as the Robot, other components make it run.

Control center

The objective of the control room is to provide Robot management capabilities. It monitors and controls a Robot's operation in a network. It can be used to start/stop Robots, make schedules for them, maintain and publish code, redeploy Robots to different tasks, and manage licenses and credentials.

RPA platforms

The burgeoning RPA vendor market has been showing continual and steady growth. While the largest market is the US, followed by the UK, the market in **Asia Pacific Countries (APAC)** is also showing considerable progress. Successful pilot projects and increased customer satisfaction among the early adopters of RPA will encourage new players to adopt this technology. There is growing demand for RPA, especially in industries that need large-scale deployments. The major markets for RPA are banking and finance, healthcare and pharmaceuticals, telecom and media, and retail.

A few key vendors, their client market, and company specifications are mentioned in the following sections.

Automation Anywhere

Automation Anywhere helps to automate business processes for companies. They focus on RPA, cognitive data (machine learning and natural language processing), and business analytics. Their bots are capable of handling both structured as well as unstructured data. The system has three basic components:

1. *A development client* for the creation of a bot
2. *A runtime environment* for the deployment of a bot
3. *A centralized command system* for handling multiple bots, analyzing their performance:
   - **HQ**: San Jose, California, USA
   - **Est**: 2003
   - **CEO**: Mihir Shukla
   - **Some key clients**: Deloitte, Accenture, AT&T, GM, J P Morgan Chase
   - **Source of revenue by region**: Its highest source of revenue is the USA, which accounts for more than half its revenue, followed by APAC, then UK and continental Europe
   - **Source of revenue by industry**: The **Banking, Financial services, and Insurance (BFSI)** accounts for more than half of its revenue, followed by healthcare, telecom, media, and others

UiPath

UiPath is an RPA technology vendor who designs and delivers software that helps automate businesses. The RPA platform consists of three parts:

- *UiPath Studio* to design the processes
- *UiPath Robot* to automate tasks designed in UiPath Studio
- *UiPath Orchestrator* to run and manage the processes:
  - **HQ**: Bucharest, Romania
  - **CEO**: Daniel Dines
  - **Key Clients**: Atos, AXA, BBC, Capgemini, CenturyLink, Cognizant, Middlesea, OpusCapita, and SAP
  - **Source of revenue by region**: North America, Continental Europe, the UK, and APAC
  - **Source of revenue by industry**: BFSI, healthcare, telecom and media, and retail

Blue Prism

Blue Prism aims to provide automation that enterprises can use according to their needs. Blue Prism aims to do this by providing automation that is scalable, configurable, and centrally managed. It sells its software through its partners, some of which are Accenture, Capgemini, Deloitte, Digital Workforce Nordic, HPE, HCL, IBM, TCS, Tech Mahindra, Thoughtonomy, and Wipro:

- **HQ**: United Kingdom
- **Est**: 2001
- **CEO**: Alastair Bathgate
- **Key Clients**: BNY Mellon, RWE npower, and Telefonica O2
- **Source of revenue by region**: More than half of its revenue source comes from the UK, followed by North America, Continental Europe, and APAC
- **Source of revenue by industry**: BFSI, health, and pharmaceuticals, retail and consumer, telecom and media, manufacturing, public sector, travel, and transportation

WorkFusion

WorkFusion offers automation that is based on RPA and machine learning. It delivers software as a solution for automating high volume data. WorkFusion enables man and machine to work in tandem while managing, optimizing, or automating tasks:

- **HQ**: New York, USA
- **Est**: 2011
- **CEO**: Max Yangkelivich, Andrew Volkov
- **Key Clients**: Thomson Reuters, Infogroup, Citi, and Standard Bank
- **Source of revenue by region**: North America provides more than 80% of WorkFusion's revenue, followed by Europe, APAC, and MEA
- **Source of revenue by industry**: Around 90% of its revenue comes from the BFSI sector, followed by the retail and consumer sectors

Thoughtonomy

Thoughtonomy delivers software that helps automate business and IT processes. It uses Blue Prism and other automation software and customizes it:

- **HQ**: London, UK
- **Est**: 2013
- **CEO**: Terry Walby
- **Key Clients**: Atos, Fujitsu, CGI, Unite BT, and Business Systems
- **Sources of Revenue by region**: Around 70% of revenue comes solely from the UK. The rest comes from Continental Europe, North America, APAC, and the **Middle East and Africa (MEA)**
- **Sources of Revenue by industry**: A major part of its revenue comes from third-party clients, followed by BFSI, public sector, telecom, healthcare, retail, and consumer sectors

KOFAX

Kofax's Kapow RPA platform is capable of automating and delivering processes that are repetitive and rule-based. It uses Robots for extracting and consolidating information. The software platform consists of a management console to deploy and manage bots, Robot performance, and a monitoring system. This software can also group together high priority tasks that should be completed first by the Robot during times of high workload. Kofax's software, however, doesn't have machine learning:

- **HQ:** Irvine, California
- **CEO:** Paul Rooke
- **Key Clients:** Arrow Electronics, Delta Dental of Colorado, Pitt Ohio, Audi
- **Sources of revenue by region:** North America accounts for almost half of its revenue, followed by Continental Europe, APAC, and LATAM (Latin America)
- **Sources of revenue by industry:** BFSI, retail, consumer, travel, transportation, public sector, manufacturing, and healthcare

About UiPath

Headquartered in Bucharest, UiPath is an RPA vendor that provides software to help organizations automate their business processes. The company aims to do away with repetitive and tedious tasks, allowing humans to engage in more creative and inspiring activities.

UiPath was founded by Daniel Dines, who is the CEO. It has offices in London, Bucharest, Tokyo, Paris, Singapore, Melbourne, Hong Kong, and Bengaluru. With clients spread across the world, from North America to the United Kingdom, Continental Europe to Asia Pacific countries, the company has shown remarkable growth in the last year, both in terms of revenue and its workforce.

Today, its software is being widely used to automate business processes. However, the IT sector is also gradually embracing UiPath's software. Major clients of UiPath in the industry include BFSI, Telecom and media, healthcare, retail and consumer, and manufacturing.

With UiPath automation software, one can configure software Robots to mimic human action on the user interface of computer systems. The basic components of the UiPath RPA platform are in line with what was explained in *Components of RPA*, these components are necessary for enterprise deployment. The components of the UiPath platform are UiPath Studio, UiPath Robot, and UiPath Orchestrator, see the following sections.

UiPath Studio

UiPath Studio helps users with no coding skills to design Robotic processes in a visual interface. It is a flowchart-based modeling tool. Thus, automation is faster and more convenient. Multiple people can contribute to the same workflow. The presence of a visual signal that points out errors in the model, and a recorder that performs what the user executes, make modeling much easier.

UiPath Robot

UiPath Robot runs the processes designed in UiPath Studio. It works in both attended (working only on human trigger) and unattended environments (self-trigger and work on their own).

UiPath Orchestrator

UiPath Orchestrator is a web-based platform that runs and manages Robots. It is capable of deploying multiple Robots, and monitoring and inspecting their activities.

The future of automation

Throughout the history of human civilization, there has been many major turning points in innovation and discoveries that have instilled awe as well as fear in the minds of people, so much so that the word *Luddite* (used for people who were strongly opposed to the introduction of textile mills during the *First Industrial Revolution* for fear of losing their livelihoods) has now become synonymous with all people who are against new technologies, be it industrialization, automation, or computerization.

The buzzword today is the **Fourth Industrial Revolution**—the current age where technology is embedded within societies and even the human body—be it Robotics, 3D printing, nanotechnology, Internet of Things, or autonomous vehicles. This will fundamentally change the way we live, work, and interact with one another.

Technological changes and innovations are taking place today at an unprecedented pace and scope and are having an impact on many disciplines. Technological innovation has reached a stage where machines have now entered the realm of what was once considered exclusively human. For these reasons, there is a wide section of people who fear this age of Robots. While the arguments over how much of our lives will be taken over by Robots are endless, what cannot be denied is that Robots are here to stay.

There are various advantages of automation today; there are also fears surrounding its advancement, which are not completely unfounded.

As mentioned earlier, this time automation is capable of impacting a wide range of disciplines. Thus, unlike in the past where only blue collar jobs were at risk of being replaced by machines, this time even white collar jobs are believed to be at risk. While this is not untrue, reports suggest that only around 5% of the total jobs may be *totally* replaced by automation. For other jobs, automation will only replace a part of the job and not completely take over.

There are, of course, those jobs in the 5% category that run the risk of being completely automated. These are the jobs that are routine, repetitive, and predictable. A few examples are telemarketing, data entry operation, clerical work, retail sales, cashiers, toll booth operators, and fast food jobs.

However, like in the past, people should be able to find a way to adapt to the changes. With each generation, humans become smarter, more adaptable to change, and also progressive. Also, with automation mostly taking over routine and tedious tasks, humans are provided the opportunity to make better use of their capabilities—be it reasoning, emotional intelligence, or their creativity. What we can do is not fret over the inevitable rather prepare for it. One way of doing so is to start changing the pattern of education. The next generation should be taught how to recognize and adapt to changes quickly. An important aspect of their education should be to *learn how to learn*.

Summary

In this chapter, we acquired a basic understanding of RPA and the ability to differentiate it from other types of automation. We have also learned globally about the benefits of RPA and various platforms available on the market. In the next chapter, we will start learning UiPath and the recording tool, which is a quick and efficient way of implementing RPA.

2
Record and Play

The facility of recording user steps on a computer and playing them back has made **Robotic Process Automation (RPA)** highly successful. Without this feature, the adoption of the technology might have been very slow and it would have been seen as another automation/scripting tool.

In the previous chapter, we gained a basic understanding of Robotic process automation. In this chapter, we will see how to use the recorder as the first step of automation in our journey. Before that, let us understand the UiPath tool and learn how to install it (you can only use the recorder after installing it). We will cover:

- The UiPath stack and components of the platform.
- How to download and install UiPath components.
- Understanding the Project Studio in detail. The Project Studio is the place where developers spend most of their time configuring the Robots.
- The recorder, with two step-by-step examples to quickly master record and play.

UiPath stack

In order to make the UiPath platform fully operational at an enterprise level, there are various components that need to be in place. There are three basic components in UiPath:

1. UiPath Studio
2. UiPath Robot
3. UiPath Orchestrator

The UiPath platform is available in two variations:

1. **Enterprise Edition**: This edition is suitable for large companies starting their RPA projects and looking to scale their Robot deployments in the future. It is integrated with UiPath Orchestrator (we will discuss UiPath Orchestrator later). This version can be updated by visiting the UiPath website and by downloading the newest version of the UiPath platform installer. Running the installer automatically replaces all the old files without modifying any of your settings.
2. **Community Edition**: This is suitable for individual developers and small organizations with fewer employees. The Community Edition is always up-to-date, and it automatically updates itself as soon as a new version is available.

 The Community Edition can be used to learn UiPath free of cost.

Now, let us understand all three components in detail.

UiPath Studio

UiPath Studio is the development environment of UiPath. It is the primary tool to develop UiPath Robots.

It can be used to configure steps of a task or launch a full recorder to record a sequence of steps. The recording facility in the Studio is a game-changing feature for RPA tools. Its simplicity lets even nontechnical business users design/record steps of a process.

This studio lets the user configure Robots, that is, develop steps to perform tasks visually. Most of the configuration and coding in UiPath is visual. By using the drag-drop facility from the toolbox, you may write a whole sequence of workflows to perform a set of tasks by Robots. These steps look like a data flow diagram and are very easy to understand. It is one of the simplest visual flow diagramming tools. Most of the time, in an enterprise environment you will receive process maps to understand the flow of work, which you will use to develop Robots. The studio gives the same look and feel as a workflow. The designer gives you full control of the execution order and actions taken, also known as activities. An activity or action includes clicking a button, writing and reading a file, and so on.

UiPath Robot

UiPath Robot is a Windows service that can open interactive/non-interactive window sessions to execute processes or a set of steps, developed or recorded using UiPath Studio. Sometimes, it is also called an execution agent as it executes automation projects, or a runtime agent as it executes instructions generated by developing or recording processes in UiPath Studio. The most acceptable nomenclature is *Robot*.

These Robots can be controlled by Orchestrator, which is part of the Enterprise Edition. There is an option at installation to de-link these Robots from Orchestrator and work independently on the desktop. In most of our examples, we will refer to the Community Edition, which does not have Orchestrator, and the installed Robot will work independently in user mode.

When installed in user mode, these Robots have the exact same rights as the user. If you opted for Orchestrator, you can control Robots irrespective of whether it is installed on a user machine, in user mode, or on a server.

Types of Robots

The following are types of Robots:

- **Attended**: It operates on the same workstation as a human to help the user accomplish daily tasks. It is usually triggered by user events. *You cannot start a process from Orchestrator on these type of Robots, and they cannot run under a locked screen.*
- **Unattended**: It can run unattended in virtual environments and can automate any number of processes. In addition to the Attended Robot's capabilities, this Robot is responsible for remote execution, monitoring, scheduling, and providing support for work queues.
- **Free**: It is similar to Unattended Robots, but can be used *only* for development and testing purposes, not in a production environment.

These types of Robots are built to suit different automation needs, such as back or front office scenarios.

A **Front Office Robot** is another name for an Attended Robot. These Robots monitor actions along with humans. These Robots take over the work for programmed steps on a certain event such as pressing a shortcut key. There is an interaction between humans with the Robots/system to do the required work. On the other hand, Back Office Robots are Robots that have the capabilities to run unattended. They can run without interaction with humans.

UiPath Orchestrator

UiPath Orchestrator is a server-based application that lets you orchestrate your Robots, hence the name Orchestrator. It runs on a server and connects to all the Robots within the network, whether Attended, Unattended, or Free. It has a browser-based interface that enables the orchestration and management of hundreds of Robots with a click. Orchestrator lets you manage the creation, monitoring, and deployment of resources in your environment, acting in the same way as an integration point with third-party applications.

Orchestrator's main capabilities:

- It helps in creating and maintaining the connection between Robots
- It ensures the correct delivery of the packages to Robots
- It helps in managing the queues
- It helps in keeping track of the Robot identification
- It stores and indexes the logs to SQL or Elasticsearch

Behind the scenes, Orchestrator Server uses:

- IIS Server
- SQL Server
- Elasticsearch
- Kibana

We have the option to store information or logs in an SQL database or Elasticsearch (which is based on Lucene). If the size of the data is small, then SQL will be preferred. However, if we have a large chunk of data and we also need some analysis on that data, it becomes tedious. Here, text search engine tools such as Lucene come into play.

Lucene is a free and open source information retrieval software library, originally written in Java. It is a full-text search library that makes it easy to add search functionality to an application or website.

Now, you may be wondering what the role of Elasticsearch is.

Elasticsearch is built on top of the Lucene engine. It is a JSON-based architecture that can support the REST API model. Elasticsearch sends all the queries to the Lucene engine for analyzing the text, and the query is returned back to Elasticsearch. This result, in turn, is sent back to the client in JSON format.

There is another tool that is frequently used with Elasticsearch, known as Kibana, which is an open source data visualization plugin for Elasticsearch. It provides visualization capabilities on the content indexed on an Elasticsearch cluster. It is used to create bar charts, line charts, scatter plots, pie charts, and maps with large volumes of data.

The following modules exist in UiPath Orchestrator and help in managing the Robots:

- Robots
- Processes
- Jobs
- Schedules
- Assets
- Queues

Downloading and installing UiPath Studio

To learn UiPath, you need the software. Fortunately, UiPath has provided multiple options to learn and use the platform. You may get a free trial for 60 days, which is the fully working Enterprise Edition, or you may opt for the Community Edition, which is free for learning purposes. Commercial use, however, is not allowed.

 For commercial use, you need to buy licences from UiPath. To buy licences, please contact *sales@UiPath.com*. You can also contact me if you face any difficulty in obtaining commercial licences.

UiPath Community Edition is free to use in academia, nonprofits, and small businesses with an annual turnover of less than $1 million or 250 workstations. (This may change over time, so please check license agreements at the time of downloading).

The UiPath Community Edition has the following features:

- Auto update
- No server integration
- Community forum for support
- Online self-learning
- No complex installation required
- Online activation is mandatory

To get your Community Edition of UiPath Studio, type the following link in your browser: `https://www.UiPath.com/community`:

1. A **Community Edition** page opens. Click on **Get Community Edition**:

2. On the next page, you must register yourself in order to download the Community Edition. So, use the correct details and remember them because the same email will be used to activate the software. Fill in the following details: **First Name***, **Last Name***, and **Email***. Filling in the **Twitter User** field is not mandatory, but it is good to provide it:

For individuals and small professional teams.

First Name*

- Please complete this required field.

Last Name*

- Please complete this required field.

Email*

Twitter User

Example: @uipath

REQUEST COMMUNITY EDITION

Click on **REQUEST COMMUNITY EDITION**.

3. You will be directed to a page that requests you to check your email for downloading the link. Click on the link to download UiPath Studio. You may also directly download UiPath Studio. Just click on the word **here** in **download it here**, as shown in the following screenshot:

4. Once the download is complete, open the downloaded file, UiPathStudioSetup.Exe.

5. The installation will then begin. Once the installation is complete, a welcome message will be displayed. Click on the **Start Free** option:

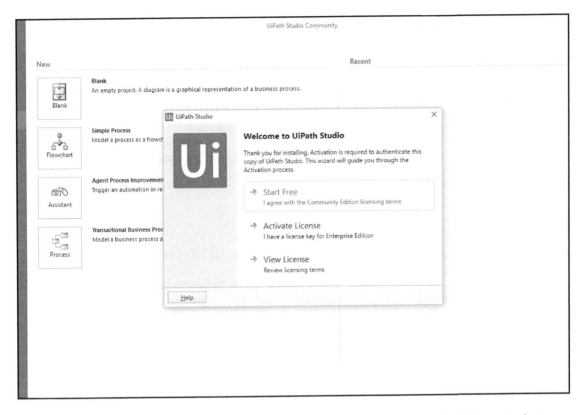

6. Then, as requested, enter your **Email Address** once again and click on **Activate**. Please remember to use the same email ID that you used to download the software. This email ID will be bound to the computer. The activation will happen online. An offline activation option is not available for the Community Edition.

7. A message will then be displayed on the screen informing you of the successful installation. Close this window.

For more convenient use, you can pin it to your taskbar immediately; otherwise, you may have to unnecessarily search for UiPath.exe in your computer every time you wish to use it.

Your UiPath Studio is now ready for use!

Learning UiPath Studio

The **UiPath Studio** platform helps to design Robotic processes with a visual interface. Automation in UiPath Studio requires no or very little prior programming knowledge. It is a Flowchart-based modeling tool. Thus, automation is faster and more convenient. The presence of a visual signal that points out errors in the model, along with the recorder, which performs what users execute, makes modeling much easier.

We will study UiPath Studio in detail now. First and foremost, let us understand the types of project available and which should be used when.

Projects

The main types of project supported by UiPath Studio are as follows:

- **Sequence**: This is suitable for simple actions or tasks. It enables you to go from one activity to another, without interfering with your project. It consists of various activities. Creating sequences is also useful for debugging purposes. One activity from a particular sequence can easily be tracked. The Basic type of project can be started using the **Blank** option in the start tab and then adding the sequence in the diagram from the toolbox.
- **Flowchart**: This is suitable for dealing with more complex projects. It enables you to integrate decisions and connect activities. To start this kind of project, choose the **Flowchart - Simple Process** option from the new project menu.
- **Assistant:** This is suitable for developing attended or Front Office Robots: sometimes these Robots are called assistants. To start this kind of project, choose the **Assistant - Agent Process Improvement** option from the new project menu.
- **State machine**: This is suitable for very large projects that use a finite number of states in their execution, triggered by a condition. To start this kind of project, choose the **Process - Transaction Business Process** option from the new project menu:

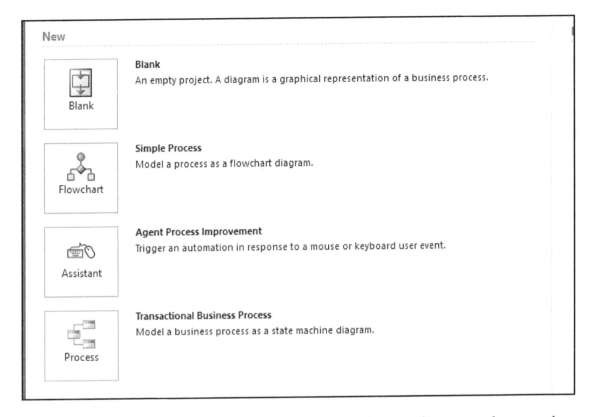

Please remember, the four types of project mentioned in the preceding screenshot are only available in the **Start** tab of the studio. However, if you click on the **New** option in the DESIGN tab, you only get three options:

- Sequence
- Flowchart
- State Machine

The preceding options selected from the DESIGN tab's **New** menu become part of an existing project and are referred to as a diagram.

UiPath Studio basically helps in automating various tasks through the designing of projects. A project is a graphical representation of any rule-based business process. It is usually in Flowchart form. One can design projects by customizing and defining the various steps, known as activities, ranging from a simple click to entering particular data.

The user interface

When you first open UiPath Studio, you are directed to the page shown in the following screenshot:

Start tab of UiPath Studio

You can either open an old project or create a new one. Let us say we are making a new project. We click on **Blank** and name it. We will then be directed to a screen, which will display the following:

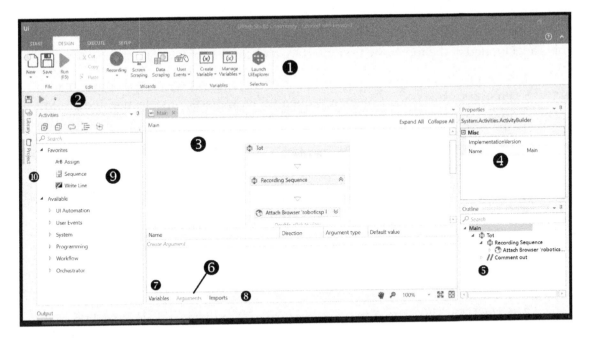

1. The Ribbon
2. Quick Access Toolbar
3. Designer panel
4. Properties panel
5. Outline panel
6. Arguments panel
7. Variable panel
8. Import panel
9. Activity panel
10. Library panel
11. Project panel
12. Output panel

The Ribbon

This panel located at the top of the user interface and consists of four tabs:

1. **START**: This is used to start new projects or to open projects previously made.
2. **DESIGN**: This is to create new sequences, Flowcharts, or state machines, or to manage variables:

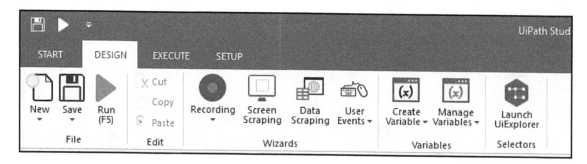

3. **EXECUTE**: This is used to run projects or to stop them, and also to debug projects:

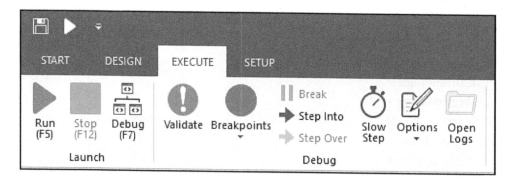

4. **SETUP**: This panel is for deployment and configuration options; it has three tools available:

- **Publish**: This is used to publish a project or create a shortcut for it and schedule tasks
- **Setup Extensions**: This is used to install extensions for Chrome, Firefox, Java, and Silverlight
- **Reset Settings**: This is used to reset all settings to defaults:

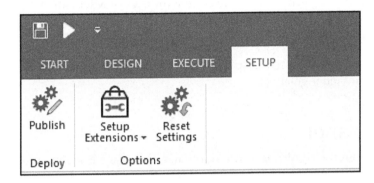

The Quick Access Toolbar

This panel gives the user a shortcut to the most used commands. One can also add new commands to this panel. This is located above the Ribbon on the user interface. The Quick Access Toolbar has been circled in the following screenshot and is indicated by the arrow:

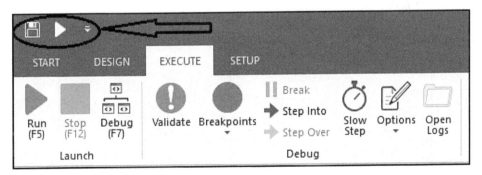

It can be moved above or below the Ribbon. By default, there are two buttons available, **Save** and **Run**, which are also available in the **DESIGN** tab of the Ribbon.

Designer panel

This is the panel where one defines the steps and activities of the projects. It is where a developer does most of the things to record activities or manually drop activities on the canvas. In UiPath, this is equivalent to the code windows of Microsoft Visual Studio. When we develop a Robot, this is the window where we will be organizing various activities in a flow or chain to accomplish a task.

The project a user makes is clearly displayed on the Designer panel and the user has the option of making any changes to it.

Properties panel

The panel located on the right-hand side of the user interface is for viewing the properties of the activities and for making any changes, if required. You need to select an activity first and then go to the **Properties** panel to view or change any of its properties:

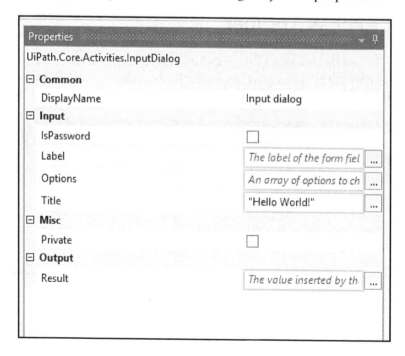

Activities panel

Located on the left-hand side of the user interface, this panel contains all the activities that can be used in building the project. The activities can easily be used in making a project by simply dragging and dropping the required activity into the required location in the Designer panel.

Project panel

With the **Project** panel, you can view the details of your current project and open it in a **Windows Explorer** window. It is located on the extreme left-hand side of the design panel, below the **Library** panel:

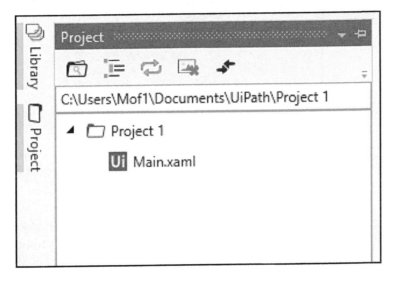

Outline panel

As the name suggests, this panel gives a basic outline of the project. The activities that make up the workflow are visible in this panel. Using this, you may see a high-level outline of the project and you can drill down to see deeper. This panel is especially helpful of large automation projects, where one may otherwise have a tough time going through it:

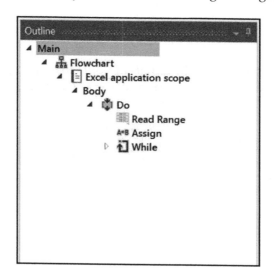

Output panel

This panel displays the output of the *log message* or *write line* activities. It also displays the output during the debugging process. This panel also shows errors, warnings, information, and traces of the executed project. It is very helpful during debugging. The desired level of detail can be changed in **Execute | Options | Log activities**:

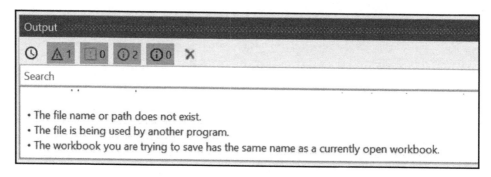

Library panel

With this panel, you can reuse automation snippets. It is located on the extreme left-hand side of the Designer panel:

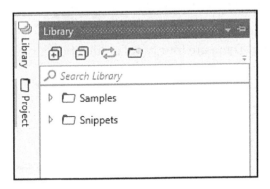

Variable panel

This allows the user to create variables and make changes to them. This is located below the Designer panel.

In UiPath Studio, variables are used to store multiple types of data ranging from words, numbers, arrays, dates, times, and timetables. As the name suggests, the value of the variable can be changed.

An important point to note is that variables can only be created if there is an activity in the Designer panel.

To create new variables, you can go to the **DESIGN** tab on the Ribbon and click on **create variable**, then choose the type of variable. Otherwise, one can simply go to the Variable panel located below the Designer panel and create a variable. Also, if one renames a variable in the Variables panel, the variable is renamed in every place it is used in the workflow. The Scope of the variable shows where the variable is located.

Argument

While variables pass data from one activity to another in a project, arguments are used for passing data from one project to another. Like variables, they can be of various types—String, Integer, Boolean, Array, Generic, and so on.

Since arguments are used to transfer data between different workflows, they also have an added property of *direction*. There are four types of direction:

- In
- Out
- In/Out
- Property

These depend on whether we are giving or receiving data to or from another workflow.

Task recorder

The task recorder is the main reason for RPA's success. With the task recorder, we can create a basic framework for automation. The user's actions on the screen are recorded by the recorder and turned into a recording sequence in the current project. That's how Robots are able to mimic human actions.

The recording is collection of execution steps that has to be taken, on the applications in the scope, in order to accomplish a task.

These steps can be recorded one by one (manually) by pointing it on the screen or many steps in a go that is, automatically.

There are four types of recording in UiPath Studio:

- Basic
- Desktop
- Web
- Citrix

We will talk about them later. The user can modify the recorded sequence even after the recording is over. This is especially helpful in cases where small changes have to be made to the recording sequence. The option to modify an existing recorded sequence thus ensures that there is no need to record the entire process again.

There are four basic types of recording:

- **Basic recorder**: Basic recorder is used to record activities on the desktop. This type of recorder is used for single activities and simple workflows. The actions here are self-contained and not contained in separate windows, as shown in the following screenshot:

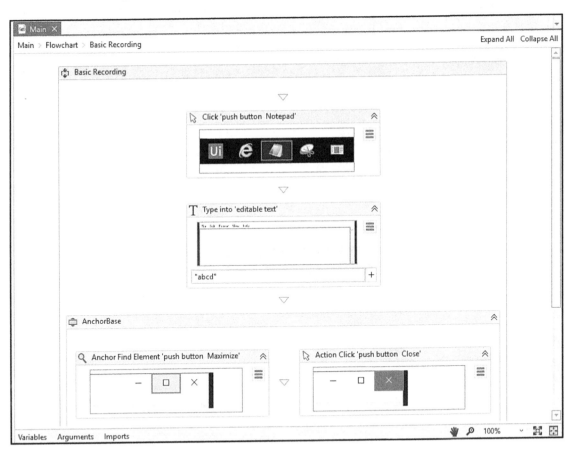

- **Desktop recorder**: The desktop recorder, like the basic recorder, is used to record activities on the desktop. However, it is used to record and automate multiple actions and complex workflows. Each activity here is contained in an **Attach Window** component, as shown in the following screenshot. The **Attach Window** component is especially important to ensure that other windows of the same application do not interfere in the workflow. UiPath uses the name of the app, the title of the window, and the currently opened file to locate and identify the correct window. However, there may be cases where, for example, two untitled Notepads are open on the screen. Without **Attach Window**, UiPath may select the wrong Notepad, thus causing errors:

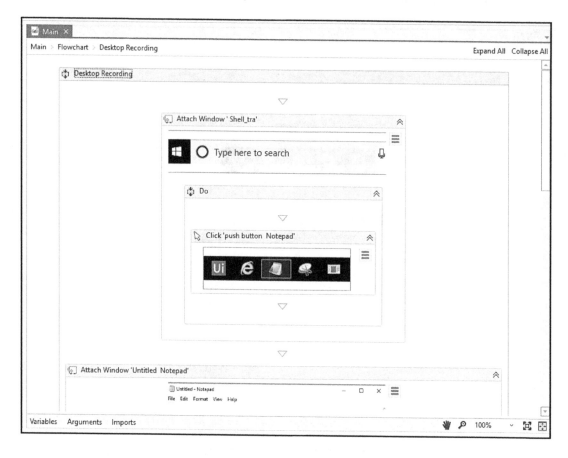

- **Web recorder**: The web recorder, as the name suggests, is used to record actions on web applications and browsers.
- **Citrix recorder**: Citrix is used to record virtual machines, VNC, and Citrix environments. This recording allows only keyboard, text, and image automation.

Some actions are recordable while others are not:

- **Recordable actions**: Left-click on buttons, check boxes, drop-down lists, and other GUI elements. Text typing is also recordable.
- **Actions that cannot be recorded**: Keyboard shortcuts, mouse hover, right-click. Modifier keys such as *Ctrl* and *Alt* cannot be recorded.

There are two types of recording:

- **Automatic recording**: This is for recording multiple actions in one go. This is a very good feature for preparing a solid foundation for automating a task. It can be invoked with the **Record** icon available in basic, desktop, and web recorders. The Citrix recorder does not support automatic or multiple step recording. A few types of action cannot be recorded using automatic, for example, hotkeys, right-click, double-click, and a few more. For all these activities, you should use a single step recorder, also know as a manual recorder.
- **Manual recording**: This type of recording is used to record each step one at a time and hence offers more control over the recording. Also, it can record all actions that cannot be recorded using automatic recording such as keyboard shortcuts, mouse hover, right-click, modifier keys, such as *Ctrl* and *Alt*, finding text from apps, and many other activities.

While the desktop, basic, and web recorders can automatically record multiple actions and manually record single actions on the screen, the Citrix recorder can only record a single action (manual recording).

Shortcut keys:

- *F2* key: This pauses the recording for 3 seconds. The countdown menu is also shown on the screen.

- Right-click: Exits the recording.

- *Esc* key: Exits the recording. If one presses the *Esc* key again, then the recording will be saved.

Let us now explore the functions of these recordings. The operations that can be completed with the help of recording are as follows:

- Click (clicking a UI element: button, image, or icon)
- Type (typing any value into the available text field)
- Copy and paste

We can see a **Recording** icon at the top of the user interface on the **DESIGN** tab of the Ribbon, as shown in the following screenshot:

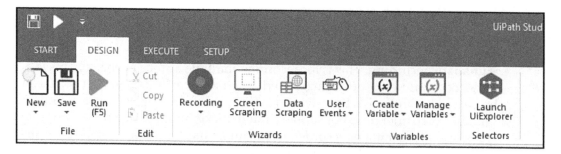

After clicking on this **Recording** icon, a list of the recording types are displayed, as shown in the following screenshot:

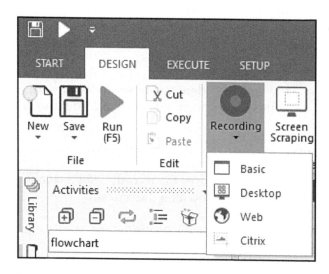

Clicking on each type of recording will result in the display of a recording panel with features specific to the type of recording. When clicking on **Basic** from the recording options, then the recording panel that appears looks as follows:

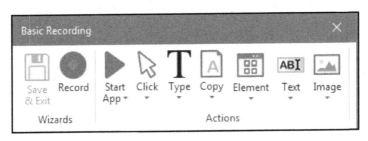

The panel that appears in the previous screenshot contains features specific to **Basic** Recording. For example; **Start App**, **Click**, **Type**, **Copy**, and so on.

- **Start App**: This is used to start an application. When we left-click on this option, we are asked to point to an application that we want to open. When we are done, we can click on the **Save & Exit** option. The following screenshot shows the recorded sequence.

    As we can see in the screenshot, an open `explorer.exe` program appears. This is the title of the application. Below it, the path of this application is shown. As mentioned previously, the features that appear in the panel are specific to the type of recording. In case of web recording, there is an option of **Open Browser** rather than **Open Application**:

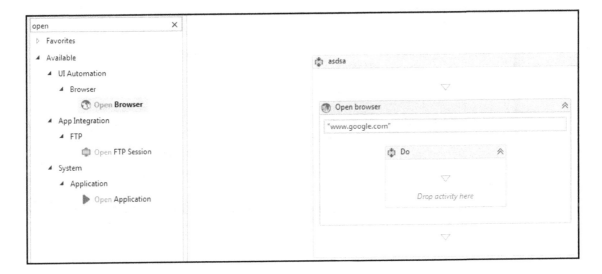

- **Click**: Another option is **Click**, which is used to click on a UI element. This feature is used as a mouse input. That is, it is used for clicking, checking, or selecting an item. When we click on this option, we are asked to indicate the location of the UI element we want to click. We can change the type of click to right-click or double-click in the **Click Type** property from the **Properties** panel.

- **Type**: Another option shown in the recording panel is Type. As the name suggests, it is used for typing something inside the indicated element. Say, for example, you want to type something in Command Prompt. All you need to do is to indicate the area where you want to type. Then, you need to type your input in the popup that appears for typing. Checking the empty field box (shown in the following screenshot) ensures that text written in the past (if any) will be emptied, leaving you with only the current text you have typed:

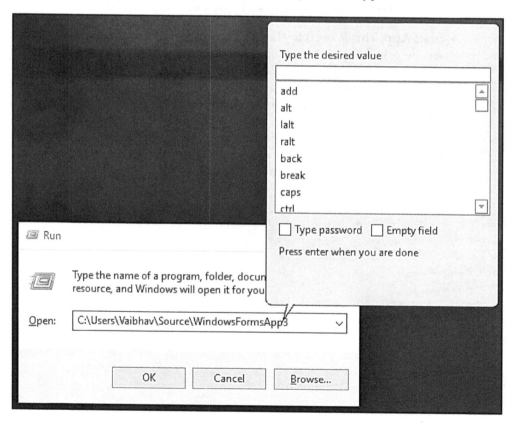

After you are done typing, do not forget to press the *Enter* key. When the *Enter* key is pressed, the step is recorded. You can then click on **Save & Exit** to view the recording sequence.

The recording sequence is shown in the following screenshot. You can change the text you have written (by changing the value of the **Type** in the block). You can write the desired text in double quotes (" "), or you can simply use a variable to store the data:

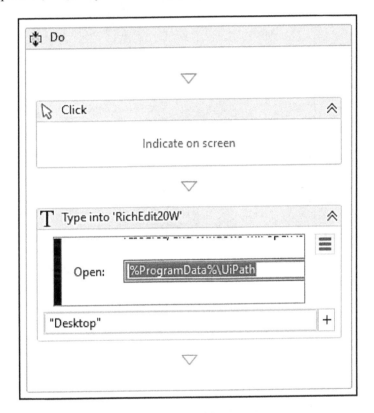

- There are three more options in the recording panel:

    - Element
    - Text
    - Image

These three are UI elements; the same keyboard and mouse options can be performed on them as explained in the preceding screenshot.

- You can see by clicking on the **Element** option that the click and type options are available as shown in the following screenshot:

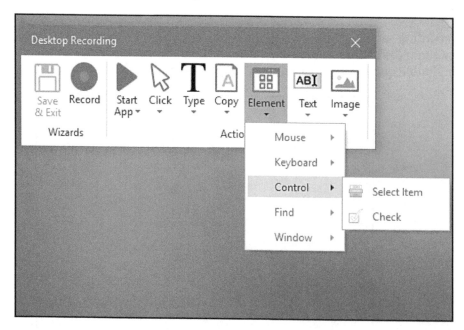

Similarly, in case of **Text** and **Image** options, there are basically two events that come into play:

- Clicking any text or image indicated as the UI element

- Get text or get image

Advanced UI interactions

Advanced UI interactions are input and output interactions. In other words, it refers to the types of input methods and output techniques that are used while automating.

Input methods

The input that we give in the form of text can be of three types:

1. Default
2. Simulate
3. Window message

Default is the generated method, while the other two are available in the **Properties** panel.

There are two checkboxes for these two methods. The Default method is the slowest process and is the best way to test whether our input option is working or not.

The other two methods work in the background. Out of these three methods, the simulate type is the fastest method and is mostly preferred because in the window message input type, it types only the lowercase characters.

Output methods

These are the methods we use for getting our output, which can be in the form of text or images. The available methods are:

- Native
- Full text
- OCR

Native is, by default, the generated method to extract data from the window. When you indicate to any element, the scraping window appears, and here all of the options can be found. We can choose any one that displays better results. OCR is preferred when the other two fail to extract data:

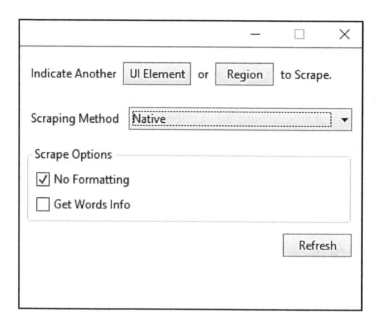

As shown in the screenshot, the scraping methods are **Native**, **Full text**, and **OCR**.

 In OCR, there are two types of **OCR engine**: One is Google OCR and the other is Microsoft OCR. We can choose whichever displays better results. Also, we can adjust the scale mentioned in the properties of the OCR. This scale can be used to improve the efficiency of the OCR.

Step-by-step examples using the recorder

In this section, we will illustrate two examples of using the UiPath recorder:

1. Emptying the trash folder in Gmail
2. Emptying Recycle Bin

The first one is to show a recording of a web-based application, and the second is Windows-based. These are very simple examples, and show how a simple task can be automated quickly.

Emptying trash in Gmail

This is an example of how we can empty a folder in Gmail with the help of a UiPath Robot, solely on the basis of recording.

 To do this, we are going to record all the actions that have to be performed to empty this Trash folder so that our Robot understands the sequence to be performed.

We can see the process flow of this simple activity in the following diagram:

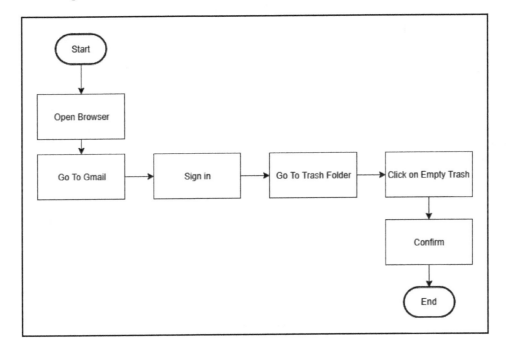

Process flow for emptying Gmail trash

We need to see all process flows, however small or big, as shown in the previous diagram. This makes developing RPA much easier and, organized.

First and foremost, we begin with a blank project in UiPath Studio and then choose **Web** recorder from the **Recording** drop-down list:

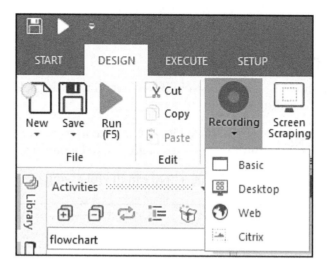

We have to click on the **Recording** option and select the type of recording. As discussed before, we will use **Web** recording for this process since we are working on a website. Just click on the **Recording** icon at the top of the page. From the four types of recording that appear, choose **Web** recording. A **Web Recording** panel will appear, as shown in the following screenshot:

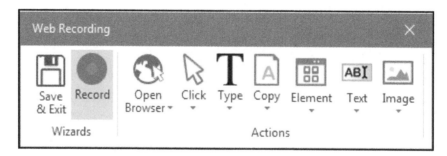

Notice **Open Browser** between **Record** and **Click**; this is available with web recorder to record steps in browser-based applications.

Preparation: Open your favorite browser, navigate to `https://gmail.com`, and keep this browser open.

The following are the six steps in our process flow:

1. **Open Browser**: Although we have already opened Gmail in the browser, we did not record that step. Here, we will note that step in the recorder using the **Open Browser** button in the recorder. A drop-down menu will appear. Again, choose **Open Browser** from the drop-down menu. It will ask to highlight the browser, highlight the already opened browser and click on the top of the browser.

2. **Go to gmail.com**: You will be prompted to enter the **URL** of the website to navigate to. Type `https://gmail.com` or `gmail.com` and press **OK**:

Please remember the first step will merely make note of the steps in the recording but will not do anything on the screen. From the next step onwards, we will use the already opened `gmail.com`.

3. **Sign In**: Start recording by clicking on the **Record** icon of the recording panel.

Go to the already open Gmail and click on the Email or Phone field. UiPath will pop up a prompt for typing the email:

Type Email in the box provided by the UiPath recorder and press *Enter*. The Gmail textbox will automatically fill up with your typed content.

Click on the **NEXT** button of the Gmail interface; it will also get recorded.

Now, you have recorded an entry in the password field. For simplicity, you may type the password in the prompt provided by UiPath.

In a real-world environment, you will select the **Type password** checkbox if you are entering a password (details on this will be discussed in later chapters).

Type your password in the text field of the popup that appears. Then, click **NEXT** to log in to your account. Clicking on the **NEXT** button will also get recorded.

4. **Locate Trash Folder**: In this step, we have to click on the search box of Gmail and type in:trash in the UiPath prompt and hit *Enter*:

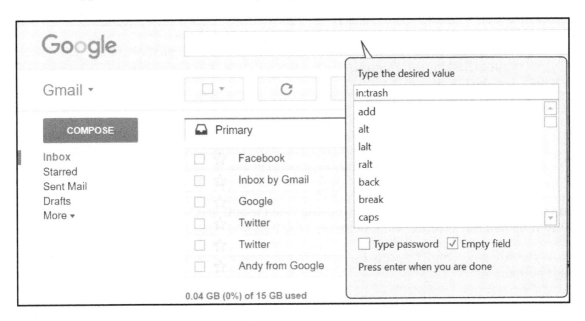

Now, click on the Search button beside the search box. It will also get recorded automatically and the Trash folder will appear.

5. **Click on Empty Trash now**: Once you are done with clicking on the Trash action, You can see a link showing **Empty Trash now**. Hover mouse on this link and it will get highlighted, click on it to delete all the messages in the Trash folder:

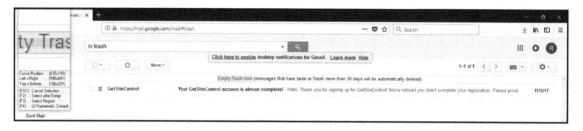

6. **Confirm**: When you click on **Empty Trash now**, a confirmation dialog will appear asking your permission for the action. Just confirm your action by clicking on the **OK** button.

 After clicking on any button, the recorder may display a dialog for using the **Indicate Anchor**. In that case, just click on the **Indicate Anchor** button and indicate the element adjacent to the button you want to click. This is used to confirm the location of the element on which you are performing the action.

In the indicate anchor wizard, we have to indicate the adjacent button, that is, the **Cancel** button, so that the recorder will identify that the button is adjacent to **Cancel**.

Now recording is complete, press *Esc* to get to the recording dialog. Click on the **Save & Exit** button.

Then, in UiPath Studio, you can see a recording sequence in the Designer panel. Rename it to `emptying trash folder`. This will help in easy recognition of the purpose of the sequence.

Now run it by pressing the *;F5* key; it should perform the same task again. You have created your first Robot, which empties trash from your Gmail!

Emptying Recycle Bin

We are going to automate emptying the Recycle Bin. There are various steps that are involved. Let's map the process of how to empty the Recycle Bin:

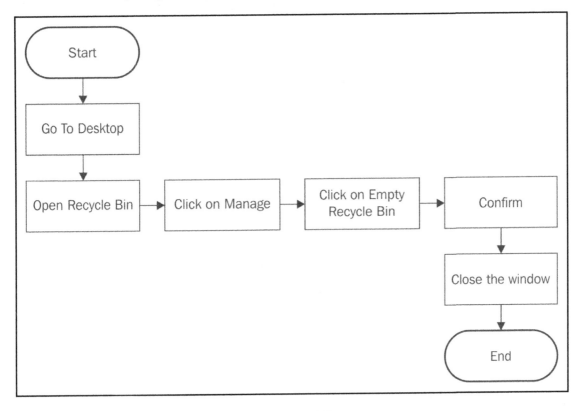

Steps to empty Recycle Bin

This diagram is simpler and more detailed than in the Emptying trash in Gmail example; we need to do exactly the same steps in order to perform this task.

Open UiPath Studio and choose a blank project. Since we are working in the recorder, and since we are working on the desktop and not a web application, we are required to choose the **desktop** recorder:

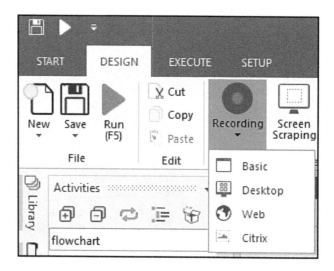

Start the recorder and simply perform the following steps:

1. Go to the desktop by pressing the *Windows + D* keys.
2. Open Recycle Bin by clicking on Recycle Bin and then pressing *Enter* key.
3. Click on the **Manage** tab of the `Recycle Bin` folder.
4. Click on the **Empty Recycle Bin** button.
5. Confirm by clicking on the **Yes** button in the dialog box.
6. Close the Recycle Bin folder by pressing the **cross** button.
7. Press the *Esc* key and **Save & Exit** the recorder.

Now your recording is ready to view, let's examine each step recorded:

1. Go to the desktop by pressing *Windows + D* keys: This step is not recorded! Never mind, it is not needed. Please note that the recorded steps attach themselves to an application, and execute commands for that application, so the next step (Open Recycle Bin) will be executed on the desktop whether you are there or not.
2. Open Recycle Bin by clicking on Recycle Bin and then pressing the *Enter* key—We can see the recorded step in the following screenshot:

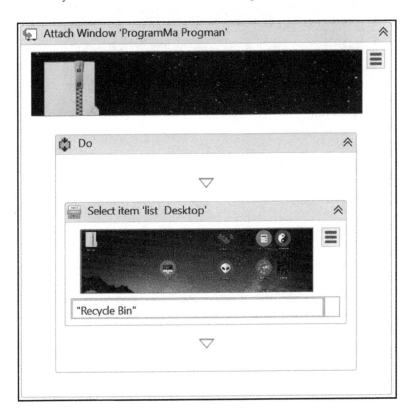

Please note that only selecting the Recycle Bin is recorded, not the *Enter* key. We should manually add that step. Search for `Send hotkey` in the **Activities** window and insert it into the workflow just below the **Select item 'list Desktop'** step, as shown in the following screenshot:

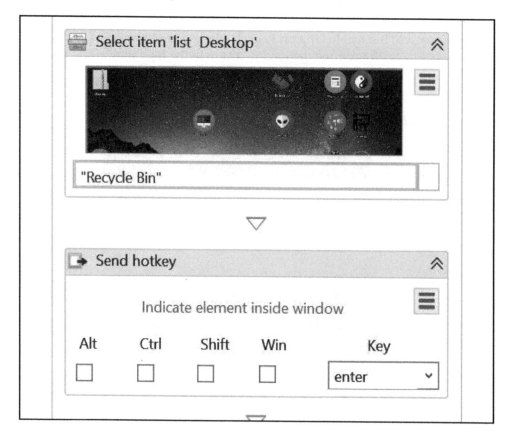

3. Click on the **Manage** tab of the Recycle Bin folder: This is recorded as it is and so is the fourth step, click on the **Empty Recycle Bin** button:

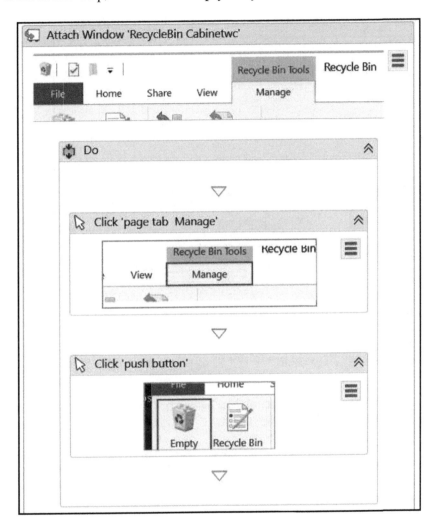

4. Confirming by clicking on the **Yes** button on the dialog box is also recorded smoothly:

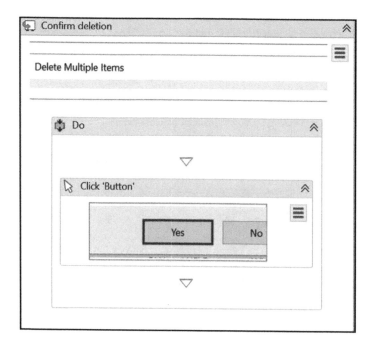

In the last step, closing the Recycle Bin folder by pressing the **cross** button, you may have to indicate an anchor.

Save it and press *F5* to run it. Voila! It runs like a charm. You see how easy it is to record steps taken on a computer and automate them.

In some scenarios, the second step of opening Recycle Bin may get recorded as a single-click instead of Selection; in that scenario, you may not manually insert **Send hotkey** for *Enter* but instead, change the single click Recycle Bin activity from single to double. For that, open your recording sequence and find the click Recycle Bin activity.

Now click this activity, and you will see that its properties contain the click activity, and we have to change the **ClickType;** from single to double.

Summary

In this chapter, we have learned about components of the UiPath platform and their functions. In the next chapter, readers will examine the project that we generated with the recorder, explain the structure of the program flow (workflow), and understand the use of sequences and the nesting of activities. Readers will learn how to use the building blocks of a workflow Flowchart and control flow (looping and decision making).

3
Sequence, Flowchart, and Control Flow

So far we have learned what RPA is, and we have seen how simple it is to *train* a UiPath Robot by recording the activities of a task and running it. Automating mundane routine tasks is very easy with UiPath using the recorder. Before we start automating complex tasks, let us learn how to control the flow of activities from one to another.

In this chapter, we will learn about methods to lay down activities in an orderly fashion and how to control the flow. These are basic to any kind of programming. We will learn about putting activities in Sequences, Flowcharts, and loops. We will also look at logical control using if-else.

To train robots to process a type of transaction, it is very important to have the instructions in a methodical flow. Mostly, these instructions are executed in Sequences. Let us understand this in detail.

This chapter will cover the following topics:

- Sequencing the workflow
- Activities
- What Flowcharts are and when to use them
- Control Flow, various types of loops, and decision making
- Step-by-step example using a Sequence and Flowchart

Sequencing the workflow

UiPath provides four types of projects:

- Sequences
- Flowcharts
- User Events
- State Machines

These are used to design a project on the basis of type and convenience. These four types of projects are useful in dealing with different kinds of processes. A Flowchart and Sequence are mainly used for simple automation. User Events are beneficial for implementing front office robots, while State Machines are used for dealing with complex business processes.

What is a Sequence?

A Sequence is a group of logical steps. Each step represents an action or a piece of work. A Sequence is used for processes that happen in linear succession, that is, one after the other. Among the three types of projects in UiPath, Sequences are the smallest. An illustration of how to build a Sequence in UiPath Studio is presented in the following section.

In the following example, we will make a simple project that asks for the name of the user and then displays his or her response:

1. Open UiPath Studio and click on **Blank** to start a fresh project. Give it a meaningful name. On the Designer panel, drag and drop a **Flowchart** activity from the **Activities** panel.
2. Search for Sequence in the **Activities** panel and then drag and drop it into the **Flowchart**, as shown in the following screenshot:

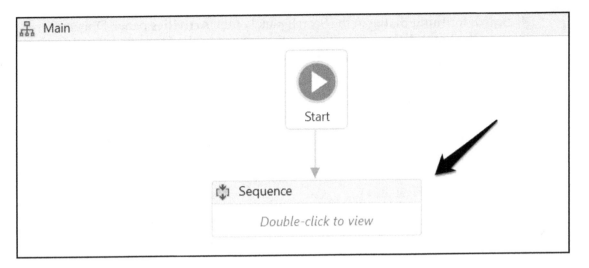

3. Double-click on the **Sequence**. We now have to add the steps that we want to perform. Consider each step as an action.

   We can add many steps inside a **Sequence**. For the sake of simplicity, we will add two steps:

   1. Ask for the username in an **Input dialog**
   2. Display the username in a **Message box**

4. Search for **Input dialog** in the Search panel of the **Activities** panel. Drag and drop the **Input dialog** activity inside the **Sequence** (the **Input dialog** activity is a dialog box that appears with a message or a question, in response to which the user is required to put in his or her reply):

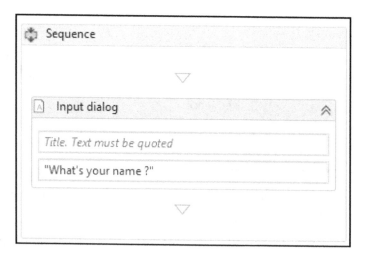

Write the appropriate message on the **Label** of this **Input dialog** to ask for the user's name. In our case, we have put in `"What's your name?"`.

5. Drag and drop a **Message box** activity into the **Sequence**. (A **Message box**, as the name suggests, displays a given text. In this case, we will use it to display the text/reply that the user has given in the **Input dialog** box on being asked his/her name.)

6. Next, create a variable and give it the desired name. This variable will receive the text that the user has entered in the **Input dialog** box in response to our question, that is, the user's name:

7. We now have to specify the **Result** property (in the **Properties** panel) of the **Input dialog** box. On specifying the variable name there, it will receive the text that the user entered. Click on the dotted icon that appears on the right side of the **Result** property. Now, specify the variable name:

8. Specify the variable name that we have created in the Text area of the **Message box** (the Text area of the **Message box** is used to input text that will be displayed in the **Message box**). We just need to connect the **Sequence** to the **Start** icon. This can be done by right-clicking on the **Sequence** activity and choosing the **Set as Start node** option.

9. Hit the **Run** button and see the result.

Activities

In UiPath Studio, an **activity** represents the unit of an action. Each activity performs some action. When these activities combine together, it becomes a process.

Every activity resides on the **Activities** panel of the main Designer panel. You can search for a particular activity and use it in your project. For example, when we search for **browser**, all the browser activities will appear in the **Activities** panel, as shown in the following screenshot:

Using activities with workflows

We have seen how we can easily search for a particular activity. Now, let us see how to use them in a workflow:

1. Search for Flowchart in the same way that we have searched for the browser activities in the **Activities** panel search bar. Drag and drop the **Flowchart** activity inside the Designer panel.

2. The **Flowchart** appears in the Designer panel and we have a given **Start** node. The **Start** node specifies where the execution begins.

3. We are ready to use different activities in our **Flowchart**. You can use any activity/activities inside the **Flowchart**. For the sake of simplicity, let us just use a **Write line** activity.

4. Drag and drop the **Write line** activity inside the **Flowchart**. Set its text property by providing a string value. Connect this **Write line** activity with the **Start** node by right-clicking on the **Write line** activity and selecting **Set as Start Node**.

You may be wondering what the role of a workflow is. Suppose you have a big project that consists of hundreds of activities. How will you debug it? It is a developer's nightmare to deal with such a situation. Here, the workflow comes into play. To build such a big project, a developer will simply divide it into smaller modules and extract it as a workflow. Now, each workflow can be tested separately. Thus, it is very easy to find bugs and errors. Creating different workflows and combining them into a logical **Sequence** will enhance our code quality, maintainability, reliability, and readability.

We have made a smaller module and now it is time to extract it as a workflow. Right-click on the main Designer panel and choose **Extract as Workflow**:

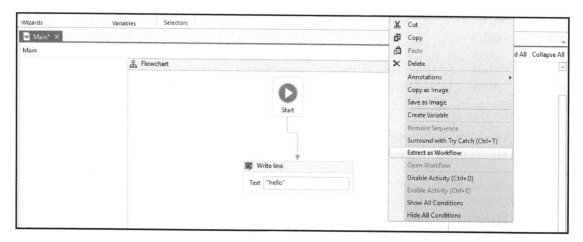

A window will pop up asking for the name. Give it a meaningful name and click on **Create**. This will be the name of your workflow:

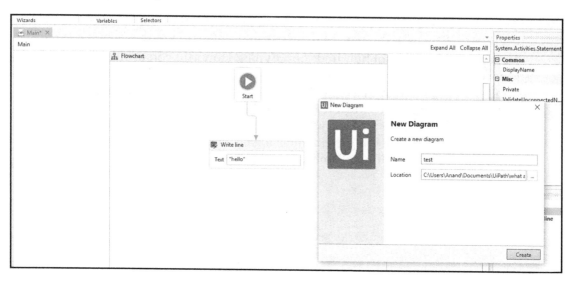

We have just used activities and extracted them in a workflow. If you check the main Designer panel, it looks like the following screenshot:

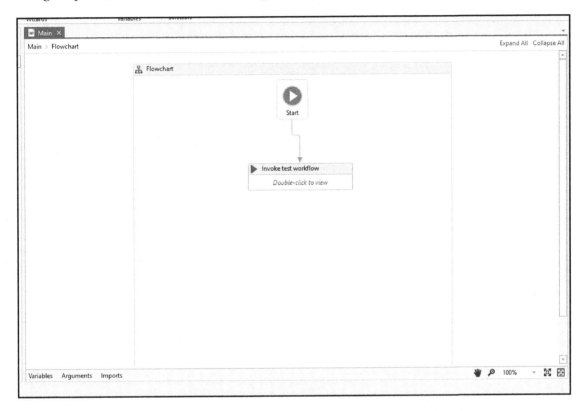

It automatically generates the **Invoke test Workflow** activity. Now, when we run the program, it will invoke the workflow that we have extracted (double-click on the **Invoke test workflow** activity to see which workflow it is going to invoke and where it is generated).

What Flowcharts are and when to use them

A Flowchart is generally used for complex business processes. It provides decision-making facilities and can be used for both small and large projects. Here, we can add activities in different ways:

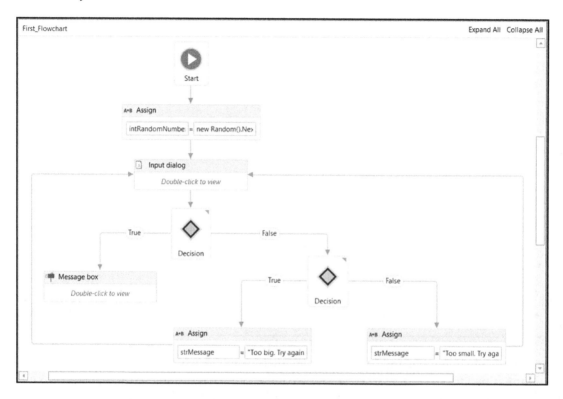

A Flowchart provides multiple branching logical operators to make decisions. A Flowchart is able to run in reverse. Also, it can be used inside Sequences. A Flowchart facilitates reusability for distinct projects. Once we create it to use in a project, it can be used for a different but similar project.

A Flowchart's branches are set to true/false by default. However, its names can be manually changed from the **Properties** panel. For example, enter two numbers and check whether their sum is less than 20.

Perform the following steps:

1. First, add a **Flowchart** from the **Activities** panel into the Designer panel.
2. Add a **Sequence** activity within the **Flowchart**.
3. Take two **Input dialog** activities (for entering the numbers to be added) inside the **Sequence** activity.
4. Create the variables x and y to save the values.
5. Next, add a **Message box** activity to perform a mathematical operation. In our case, the sum of the two numbers is less than 20:

$$x + y < 20$$

6. Now, add a **Flow Decision** activity to check the mathematical operation.
7. If true, the **Flow Decision** will flow toward the true branch. Otherwise, it will flow towards the false branch.

Control flow, various types of loops, and decision making

Control flow refers to the order or the particular manner in which actions are performed in an automation. UiPath provides numerous activities for performing the decision-making process. These activities, present in the **Activities** panel, are put into the workflow either using the double-click method or the drag and drop method.

Different types of control flow activities are as follows:

- The Assign activity
- The Delay activity
- The Break activity
- The While activity
- The Do While activity
- The For each activity
- The If activity
- The Switch activity

The Assign activity

The **Assign** activity is used to designate a value to the variable. The Assign activity can be used for different purposes, such as incrementing the value of a variable in a loop, or using the results of a sum, difference, multiplication, or division of variables and assigning it to another variable.

The Delay activity

The **Delay** activity, as the name suggests, is used to delay or slow down an automation by pausing it for a defined period of time. The workflow continues after the specified period of time. It is in the hh:mm:ss format. This activity plays a significant role when we need a waiting period during automation, perhaps say, a waiting period required for a particular application to open.

Example

To better understand how the **Delay** activity works, let us see an example of an automation that writes two messages to the **Output** panel with a delay of 50 seconds.

Perform the following steps:

1. First, create a new **Flowchart**.
2. Add a **Write line** activity from the **Activities** panel and connect it to the **Start** node.
3. Select the **Write line** activity. Now, type the following text into the **Text** box: `"Hey, what is your name?"`.
4. Next, add a **Delay** activity and connect it to the **Write line** activity.
5. Select the **Delay** activity and go to the **Properties** panel. In the **Duration** field, set 00:00:50. This is a 50-second delay between the two logged messages.
6. Take another **Write line** activity and connect it to the **Delay** activity. In the **Text** field, write `"My name is Andrew Ng."`:

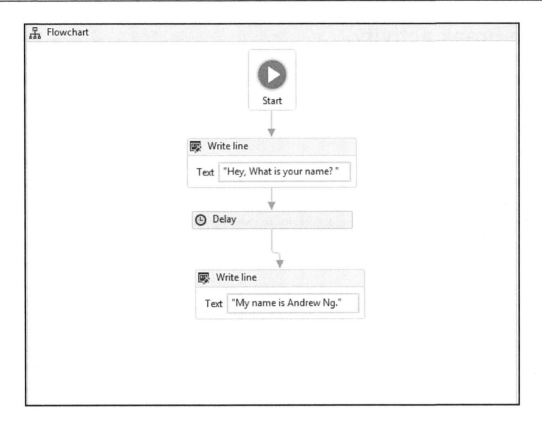

7. After clicking on the **Run** button, the **Output** panel shows the message that delays it by 50 seconds:

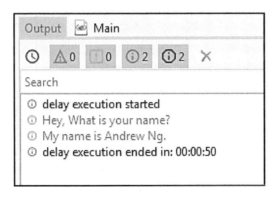

The Break activity

The **Break** activity is used to break/stop the loop at a particular point, and then continue to the next activity according to the requirement. It cannot be used for any other activity apart from the For each activity. It is useful when we want to break the loop to continue to the next activity in the For each activity.

Example

In this example, we will use the Break activity to execute only one iteration.

Perform the following steps:

1. Add a **Sequence** activity to the Designer panel.
2. Next, add a **For each** activity inside the **Sequence** (as mentioned in the preceding section, to use the **Break** activity, we need the **For each** activity):

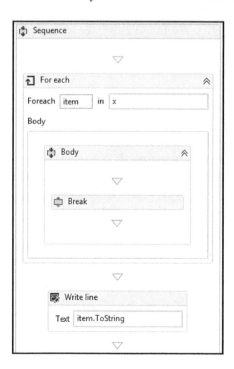

3. Create two variables; an integer variable named `item`, and an array integer variable named `x`. Then, set them to the text field.

4. Now, assign a default value to the integer variable `x`.

5. Add a **Break** activity inside the body of the loop.

6. Under the **For Each** activity, add a **Write line** activity.

7. In the **Write line** activity, type `item.ToString` in the text field.

8. When we click the **Run** button, it will display one element, as shown in the following screenshot. This is due to the **Break** activity, which has stopped execution after the first iteration:

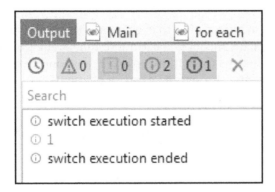

Before going on to the other control flow activities, we will learn about loops, which are an important aspect of automation. One of the most frequently mentioned advantages of automation is its ability to perform functions that are repetitive and to perform them without errors. Loops are meant precisely for such functions. Let us say, one wants to repeat a certain part of a workflow for different cases or when a certain criterion is fulfilled. In such a scenario, a loop comes in very handy. A loop can simply be created by connecting the end of the workflow to the point where we want the workflow to resume.

One thing that needs to be kept in mind while making such loops is to make sure there is also an exit point. Otherwise, the loop will continue infinitely!

The While, Do while, and For each activities mentioned among the various control flow activities are examples of loops. Let us now see where they are used and how they work.

The While activity

The While activity is used in automation to execute a statement or process based on a certain condition. If found true, the loop is executed; that is, the process is executed repeatedly. The project only exits from the loop when the condition does not hold true. This activity is useful while iterating through an array of elements.

Example

In the following example, we will see how an integer variable will increase from 5 to 50 in increments of 5.

Perform the following steps:

1. On a **Blank** project, add a **Sequence** activity.
2. Now, create an integer type variable x. Set its default value to 5.
3. Next, add a **While** activity to the **Sequence**.
4. In the condition field, set x<50.
5. Add an **Assign** activity to the body section of the **While** loop.
6. Now, go to the **Properties** panel of the **Assign** activity and type in the text field integer variable for value field integer x+5 .

7. Drag and drop a **Write line** activity and specify the variable name x and apply `ToString` method on this variable:

8. Now, click the **Run** button. The output will display in the **Output** panel, as shown in the following screenshot:

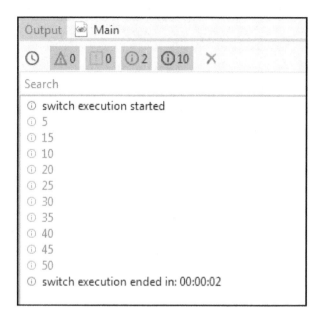

The Do while activity

The **Do while** activity is used in automation when it is required to execute a statement based on the fulfillment of a certain condition. How it differs from the While activity is that it executes a statement, then checks whether the condition is fulfilled. If the condition is not fulfilled, it exits the loop.

Example

Let us take an example to understand how the Do while activity works in automation. Take an integer variable. Starting with this variable, we shall generate all multiples of 2, less than 20.

Perform the following steps:

1. Add a **Sequence** to the Designer panel.
2. Add a **Do while** activity from the **Activities** panel.

3. In the body section of the **Do while** activity, add an **Assign** activity.
4. Now, select the **Assign** activity. Go to the **Properties** panel and create an integer variable y. Set its default value to 2.
5. Set y+2 in the value section of the **Assign** activity to increment the result each time by 2 until the loop is executed.
6. Add a **Write line** activity inside the **Assign** activity.
7. In the text field of the **Write line** activity, type y.
8. In the condition section, set the condition y<20. The loop will continue until the condition holds true:

9. On clicking the Run button, the output displayed will be as follows:

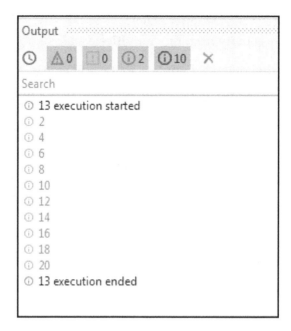

The For each activity

The **For each** activity works by iterating each element from the collection of items or list of elements, one at a time. In the process, it will execute all the actions that are available inside the body. Thus, it iterates through the data and processes each piece of information separately.

Example

In the following example, we shall use the **For each** activity to go through a collection of even numbers and display each element one at a time.

Perform the following steps:

1. Start with a **Blank** project in UiPath.
2. Add a **Sequence** activity to the Designer panel.

3. Next, add a **For each** activity within the **Sequence** and create an integer type array variable, x.

4. In the default value of the variable, put in ({2,4,6,8,10,12,14,16,18,20}).

5. Add a **Write line** activity to the Designer Panel (this activity is used to display the results).

6. In the **Text** field of the **Write line** activity, type item.ToString to display the output:

7. Now, run the program. You will see that each number of the array is displayed one by one because of the use of the **For each** activity:

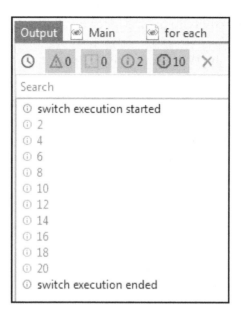

The Control flow also facilitates decision-making mechanisms that can help in taking a decision on a particular activity's step. For example, suppose we are using a loop and we want to display only a desired value, then we can filter out all our desired values by implementing the If activity, and making a decision based on the basis of the If activity's result, that is, true or false. The decision-making process will require some time to break the action after executing the desired element. This is followed by the Break activity, which will play a significant role. If you want to choose an execution from the task, then the activity needs to be switched in order to make such a decision.

The If activity and the Switch activity are the Control flow's decision-making activities.

The If activity

The If activity consists of a statement with two conditions: true or false. If the statement is true, then the first condition is executed; if not, the second condition is executed. This is useful when we have to take decisions on the basis of statements.

To better understand how the **If** activity works, let us see an example that checks whether the sum of any two numbers is less than 6.

Perform the following steps:

1. Add a **Flowchart** from the **Activities** panel.
2. Add two **Input dialog** activities. Create two integer variables, x and y.
3. In the **Properties** panel, change the label name and title name of both the **Input dialog** activities.
4. Now, specify these name of these two variables in the **Result** property of both the **Input dialog** activities.
5. Now add the **If** activity to the Designer panel:

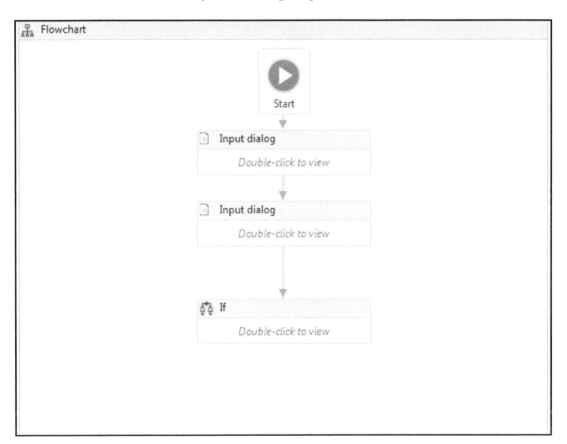

6. In the condition part, x+y<6, check whether it is true or false. Add two Write line activities and type "True" in one and "False" in the other:

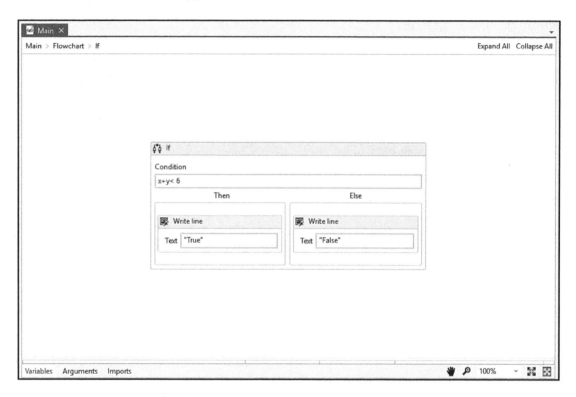

7. Click the **Run** button to check the output. If the condition holds true then it will show the true value; otherwise, it will show the false value, as shown in the second screenshot (in our case, we put in the values of *x* and *y* as 9 and 4, respectively, thus getting a sum of 13, which is not less than 6; hence, the output shows it as false value):

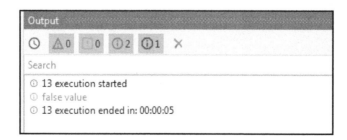

The Switch activity

The **Switch** activity can be used to make a choice. When we have various options available and want to execute one option, we frequently use the Switch activity.

By default, the Switch activity takes an integer argument. If we want to take a desired argument, then we can change it from the Properties panel, from the TypeArgument list. The Switch activity is very useful in the categorization of data according to one's own choice.

Example

Let's see an example where we have to check whether a given number is odd or even.

We know that all odd numbers, when divided by 2, leave a remainder of 1. On the other hand, even numbers, on being divided by 2, leave a remainder of 0. Hence, we will have two cases getting a remainder of 1 or 0.

Perform the following steps:

1. Add a **Sequence** activity.
2. Add an **Input dialog** activity inside the **Sequence**.
3. Now, create an integer type variable `k`.
4. Specify the newly created variable's name in the **Result** property inside the **Properties** panel.
5. Add the **Switch** activity under the **Input dialog** activity.
6. In the **Expression** field, set `k mod 2` to check whether the number is divisible by 2 or not.
7. Add a **Write line** activity to the **Default** section and type the `k.ToString +"
is an even number"`
in the text field.

8. Now, create **Case 1**, add the one other **Write line** activity to it, and type `k.ToString +" is an odd number"` in the text field:

Step-by-step example using Sequence and Flowchart

A Sequence and a Flowchart are similar concepts. They are both used to contain logical steps or actions. One should know when to use each of them. Where they differ from each other is that a Sequence is generally used to contain multiple steps to perform an action. A Flowchart, on the other hand, is suitable for a particular task. When we have lots of steps of a similar kind, we contain them in a Sequence. There may be different Sequences doing their jobs. We can easily put similar Sequences into a workflow; each workflow represents a task. It is very easy to test a separate workflow alone. Let us try to understand them better with an example.

How to use a Sequence

There may be different Sequences doing their jobs. We can easily put similar Sequences into a workflow; each workflow represents a task. It is very easy to test a separate workflow alone. Let us try to understand them better with an example.

Perform the following steps:

1. Drag and drop a **Flowchart** onto the Designer panel. Drag and drop a **Sequence** activity. Connect the **Sequence** activity with the **Start** node.
2. Double click on the **Sequence** activity. Drag and drop an **Input dialog** activity and a **Message box** activity. Specify a message in the **label** property of the **Input dialog** activity.
3. Create a variable of type **String**. Give it a name. Also, specify this newly created variable's name in the content property of the **Message box** activity:

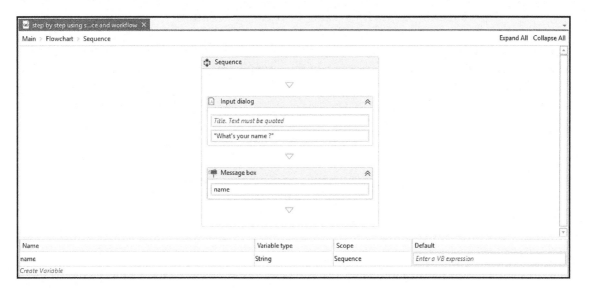

Hit the **Run** button or press *F5* to see the result.

We can see clearly that we have used two activities inside the **Sequence** that are logically related (one for inputting the name and the other for popping it up). Here, the **Sequence** contains two activities. Of course, you can put as many activities as you want inside the **Sequence**; it will be executed according to the order in which you have defined it.

How to use a Flowchart

Previously, we have seen how to use a Sequence and activities. We shall now learn how to use a **Flowchart**. A **Flowchart** is a container. It can contain activities inside it.

 I order to use email activities in example please install **UiPath.Mail.Activities**. You can find it by clicking on Manage package icon or pressing *Ctrl + P* and search for mail in all package. You will learn more on packages in Chapter 6, *Taking Control of the Controls*.

Let us drag and drop a **Message box** activity inside the **Flowchart**. Double click on the **Message box** and type `"Hello World!"` in the area where the text is to be quoted. Press *F5* to see the result):

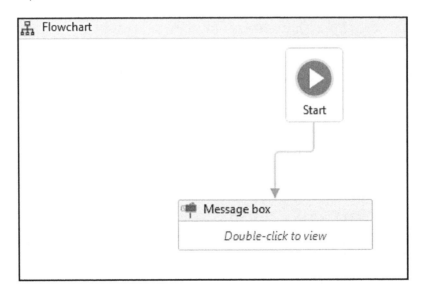

So, when the program has only a few steps, we can use activities directly inside the **Flowchart**. However, it becomes more complex when we have a large number of steps. That is why it is necessary to arrange the related activities into Sequences and then group the Sequences into a **Flowchart**.

Let us take an example to see how to use Sequences in the **Flowchart**.

 We are not going to implement the actual code for sending the email. It will be covered later in detail. The aim of this session is to clearly understand where and how we use workflows and Sequences.

Perform the following steps:

1. Drag and drop two **Flowchart** activities on the main **Flowchart**. Rename them as Send Mail and Message.

   We have two different workflows. The **Send Mail** workflow will send the mail to an email address. The **Message** workflow has the message body of that email and will ask the user for a name, message, sender, and receiver.

2. We have to implement the desired steps in both workflows.

   For that, we are using a **Sequence** inside the **Flowchart**. Double click on the **Flowchart**. Drag and drop a **Sequence** activity inside both Flowcharts. Connect the **Sequence** to the **Start** node by right-clicking on the **Sequence** and selecting the **Set as Start node** option.

3. Double click on the **Sequence** in the **Message** Flowchart. Drag and drop four **Input dialog** activities for the name, message, sender, and receiver (in this **Sequence**, we are not going to set any property of the **Message box** since the purpose of this lesson is to clearly understand where and how we use workflows and Sequences):

4. Double click on the **Send Mail Flowchart**. Double click on the **Sequence**. You can drag and drop the email activities here. (We are not going to drag any mail activity although you are free to do so. There is another chapter for that).

5. That's it. Now, go to the main **Flowchart**. Connect the **Message Flowchart** to the **Start** node. Also, connect the **Send Mail** activity to the **Message Flowchart**:

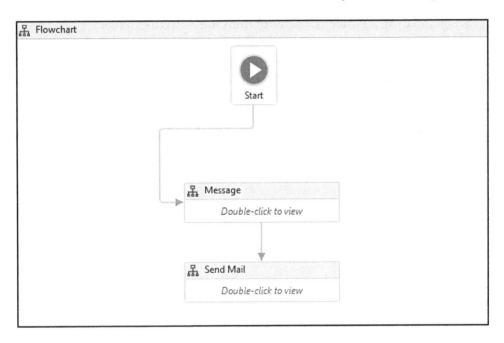

6. Run the program and visualize it.

Step-by-step example using Sequence and Control flow

In this session, we are going to discuss Control flow with an example. We will see how to use Control flow in a Sequence. There are the various Control flow activities, as mentioned before.

Consider an array of names. Say we have to find out how many of them start with the letter *a*. We will then create an automation where the number of names starting with *a* is counted and the result is displayed.

Perform the following steps:

1. Drag and drop a **Flowchart** activity from the **Activities** panel.
2. Drag and drop a **Sequence** activity inside the **Flowchart**. Connect the **Sequence** to the **Start** node by right-clicking on the **Sequence** activity and selecting the **Set as Start node** option.
3. Double click on the **Sequence** activity. Create a variable. Give it a name (in our case, we will create an array of type string and name the variable as names). Set the variable type to **Array of [T]**. When asked for the type of array, select **String**.

    Also, initialize the array in the **Default** section of the variable by giving it a default values. For example, { "John", "Sam", "Andrew", "Anita" }.

4. Create a variable of type integer **Count** for storing the result. Set the variable type to **Int32**:

5. Drag and drop a **For each** activity inside the **Sequence**. Also, specify the array name in the expression box of the **For each** activity. The **For each** activity is used to iterate over the array. It will pick up one name from the array each time until it reaches the end:

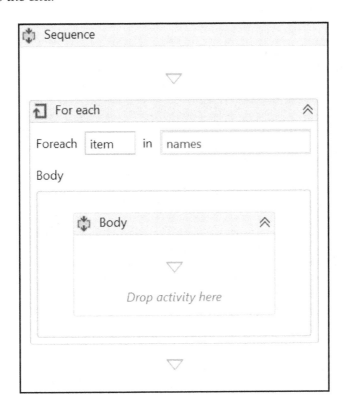

6. Drag and drop the **If** activity from the **Activities** panel and place it inside the **For each** activity at the location where *Drop activity here* is mentioned. Specify the condition in the expression box of the **If** activity. The **If** activity is used to check for a particular condition/expression. If that expression is satisfied, the **Then** block will be executed. Otherwise, the **Else** block will be executed.

We have specified the expression as `item.ToString.StartsWith('a')`. This expression specifies the name present in the item variable starts with the letter `'a'`. The **For each** activity iterates over the array, picks up one name at a time, and stores it as a variable, `item`:

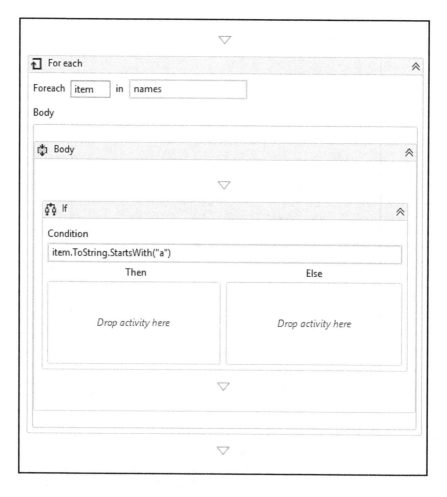

7. Now, we are going to use the Count variable and increment it each time a name from an array starts with the letter a. For this, we have to use the **A+B Assign** activity. Drag and drop the **A+B Assign** activity inside the **If** activity. Set the **To** property to Count (variable name) and the **Value** property to Count+1 (to increment its value) of the **A+B Assign** activity:

8. Just drag and drop a **Message box** activity inside the **Sequence** activity. Specify the count variable in the expression box of the **Message box** activity. But remember, the variable that we have created is of type **Int32**, so, it cannot be used with the **Message box** activity without converting it to a string. To convert it to a string, we have the '`.toString`' method available in UiPath Studio. Just apply it to the variable and select '`.toString`':

Hit the **Run** button or press *F5* and see the result.

Summary

In this chapter, we examined the project that was generated by the recorder and saw an explanation of the structure of the program flow (workflow). We understood the use of Sequences and the nesting of activities. We learned how to use the building blocks of a workflow, Flowchart, and Control flow (looping and decision making).

In the next chapter, we will learn techniques to use memory with variables, and we will also learn about using data tables to store and easily manipulate data in memory. The next chapter will also show how disk files (CSV, Excel, and so on) are used to persist data.

Data Manipulation

4

So far we have learned about the basics of RPA and how to organize steps in a workflow using a Flowchart or Sequence. We now know about UiPath components and have a thorough understanding of UiPath Studio. We used a few simple examples to make our first robot. Before we proceed further, we should learn about variable and data manipulation in UiPath. It is not very different from other programming concepts. However, here we will look at the specifics of UiPath data handling and manipulation.

This chapter will mainly deal with data manipulation. Data manipulation is the process of changing data—whether it is adding, removing, or updating it. Before learning about data manipulation, we shall see what variables, collections, and arguments are, what kind of data they store, and what their scope is. We will then carry out various examples of data manipulation. We will also learn to store and retrieve data.

In this chapter, we will cover:

- Variables and the scope of a variable in the workflow
- Collections, how to store data in arrays, and how to traverse them
- Arguments, why we need them, and how to use them
- Clipboard usage
- Data scraping
- File management with a step-by-step example
- Data table usage with an example

Variables and scope

Before discussing variables, let us take a look at **Memory** and its structure:

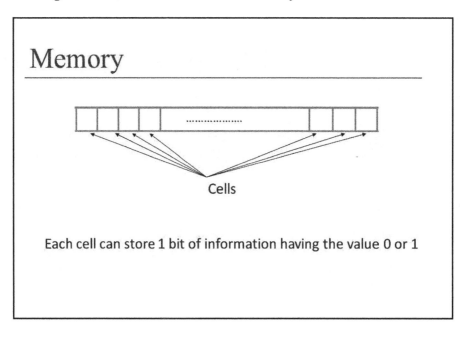

Memory consists of millions of memory **Cells** and each memory cell stores data in the form of 0s and 1s (binary digits). Each cell has a unique address, and by using this address, the cell can be accessed:

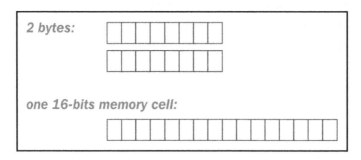

When data is stored in memory, its content gets split into further smaller forms (binary digits). As shown in the preceding diagram, **2 bytes** of data consists of several memory cells.

A variable is the name that is given to a particular chunk of memory cells or simply a block of memory and is used to hold data.

You can declare any desired name and create a variable to store the data.

It is recommended, however, that we use meaningful variable names. For example, if we wish to create a variable to store the name of a person, then we should declare

Name: Andy

It is a good practice to create meaningful variable names. This becomes very useful in debugging the program.

As we discussed, a variable is used to store data. Data is present around us in different types—it can be an mp3 file, text file, string, numbers, and so on. That is why variables are associated with their respective data types. A particular type of variable can hold only that type of data. If there is a mismatch between the data and the variable type, then an error occurs. The following table shows the type a of variable available with UiPath:

Type	Content
Integer	Whole numbers
String	Text of any kind: "The Quick Fox @4598"
Boolean	True or false
Generic	Anything

In UiPath, we can declare a variable in the **Variables** section. Just give it a meaningful name and select the appropriate type from the drop-down list.

By a meaningful variable, it is implied that the variable name should not be ambiguous. Try to make it as descriptive as possible so that the person reading the code understands the purpose of the variable. Good examples are `daysDateRange`, `flightNumber`, and `carColour`. Bad examples are `days`, `dRange`, `temp`, and `data`.

We can also specify the scope of a variable. The **Scope** is the region under which the data has its effect or availability. You can choose the **Scope** of the variable according to your requirements; try to limit it as far as possible. Please refer to the following screenshot to understand **Variables** panel:

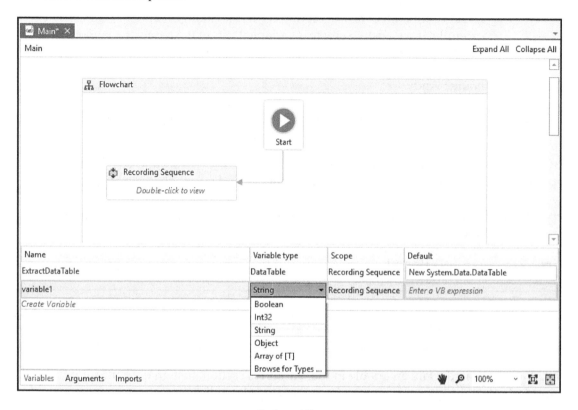

Creating a variable

 For security reasons, it is not a good practice to set the **Scope** of your variable to fullest as it may accidentally be accessed by another region or could be modified.

Let us take an example of creating a variable and then displaying a **Message box** using that variable:

1. We have declared a variable as name in the **Variables** section and set its **Default** value to "Hello world". By default, the type of the variable is **String** (we can change its type according to our needs).
2. Search for Message box in the **Activities** panel. Drag and drop that **Message box** template into a **Flowchart**.
3. Right-click on the message template and select **Set as Start node**:

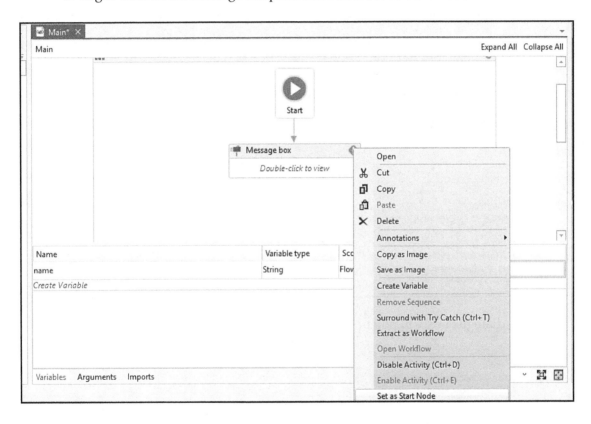

4. Double-click on the **Message box** template and specify the variable name that we created earlier. At this stage, we are ready to run our application by simply clicking on the **Run** button:

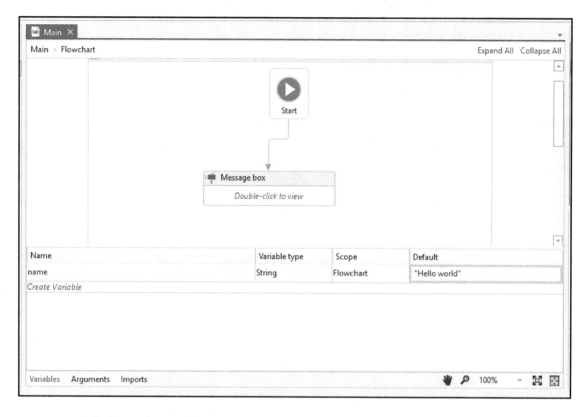

A dialogue box will pop up with the "Hello world" text displayed on it.

Collections

There are different types of variables. Variables can be classified into three categories:

- **Scalar**: These are variables that can only hold a single data point of a particular data type, for example; Character, Integer, Double, and so on.
- **Collections**: These are variables that can hold one or more data point of a particular data type. For example; array, list, dictionary, and so on.
- **Tables**: These are a tabular form of the data structure which consists of rows and columns.

In this section, we are going to see how collections work and how we can store values in the collection variables.

In a collection, we can store one or more data points, but all the data must be the same. Consider an example. An array is a collection in which we can store different values of a particular data type. It is a fixed data type, meaning if we store five values inside the array, we cannot add or remove any value/values in that array.

 The object is a data type in which you can store any type of data. Hence, if we take an array of objects then we can store different types of data in an array. This is an exceptional case.

Let us see how we can use an array with an example. In this example, we are going to take an array of integers, initialize it, and then iterate through all the elements of the array:

1. Drag and drop a **Flowchart** activity onto the main Designer panel, and drag and drop a **Sequence** activity inside the **Flowchart**. Set the sequence as **Start** node.
2. Create a variable in the **Variables** panel and give it a meaningful name (in this example, we have created a variable named arr, which is an array of integers). Choose the data type as an array of integers.

3. We have initialized the array as {1, 2, 3, 4, 5} in the **Default** section. You can initialize it with the **int32** data type:

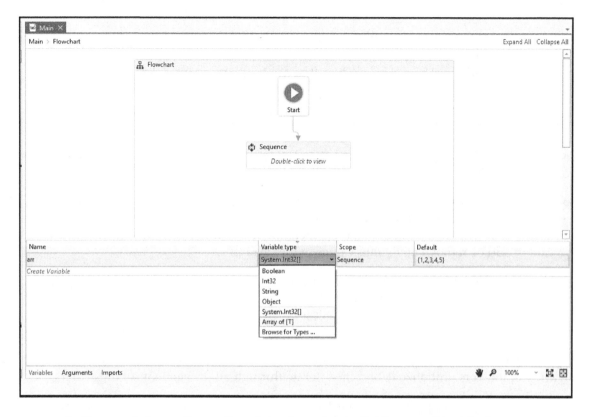

4. Drag and drop a **For each** activity from the **Activities** panel inside the **Sequence**, and drag and drop a **Message box** activity inside the **For each** activity.
5. Specify the array name in the expression text box of the **For each** activity.
6. Specify the item variable that is auto-generated by the **For each** activity, inside the **Message box** activity. But hold on, we have to convert the item variable into the **String** type because the **Message box** activity is expecting the string data type in the text box. Just press the dot (.) along with the item variable and choose the **ToString** method:

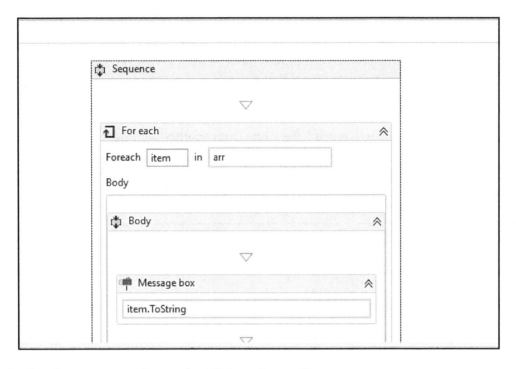

Hit the **Run** button to see the result. All the values will pop up at once.

In this example, we have seen how easily we can initialize the array and iterate through it.

Arguments – Purpose and use

An **Argument** is simply a variable that can store a value. You can create an argument in the Argument section of the main Designer panel.

But remember, they are not limited to variables. An argument has a larger scope than a variable and is used to pass values between different workflows. You might be wondering why we need this. Suppose we have a big project to build; we break down the project into different workflows because smaller workflows can be easily tested separately. It is very easy to build smaller workflows and combine them, thus turning them into the real solution of the project.

These Arguments are used for interacting with different workflows by exchanging data between them. That is why the direction property is associated with Arguments. We can choose the direction on the basis of our requirement—either giving the value to some workflow or receiving the value from another workflow.

We can easily create arguments in the **Arguments** panel. We can also specify the direction:

- **In**: When we have to receive the value from another workflow.
- **Out**: This is the current value if we have to send the value to a workflow.
- **In/Out**: This specifies both; it can take or receive the value.
- **Property**: This specifies that it is not being used currently:

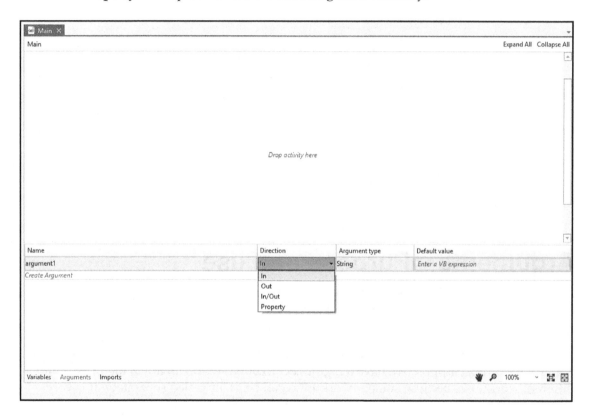

Data table usage with examples

A data table is a tabular form of data structure. It contains rows and each row has columns, for example:

Student name	Roll number	Class
Andrew Jose	1	3
Jorge Martinez	2	3
Stephen Cripps	3	2

The preceding illustration is an example of a data table that has three rows and three columns. You can build a data table in UiPath also.

A data table is used for various purposes. Say, for example, you have to build a table dynamically. You can use a data table as your preferred choice. A data table is also extensively used to store tabular data structures. In data scraping, data tables are widely used. Data scraping is a method in which we can dynamically create tabular data records of search items on the web.

We shall build two projects in which we will use a data table:

- Building a data table
- Building a data table using data scraping (dynamically)

Building a data table

Let us see, how to build a data table can be built. First, create an empty project. Give it a proper name:

1. Drag and drop a **Flowchart** activity on the Designer panel. Also, drag and drop a **Sequence** activity and set it as the **Start** node.
2. Double click on the **Sequence** and drag and drop the **Build Data Table** activity inside the **Sequence** activity.

3. Click on the **Data Table** button. A pop-up window will appear on the screen. Remove both the columns (auto generated by the **Build Data Table** activity) by clicking on the Remove Column icon:

4. Now, we will add three columns by simply clicking on the + symbol. Specify the column names and select the appropriate data types from the drop-down list. Click on the **OK** button. We will add column `Name` of **String** Data Type, `Roll_No` of **Int32** type and finally Class of string type:

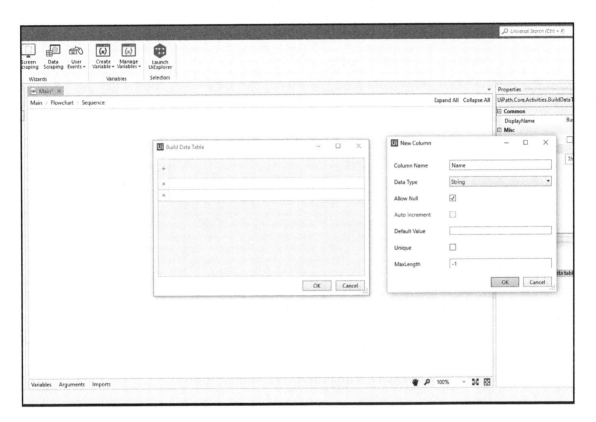

Now enter some random values just to insert the data into the rows:

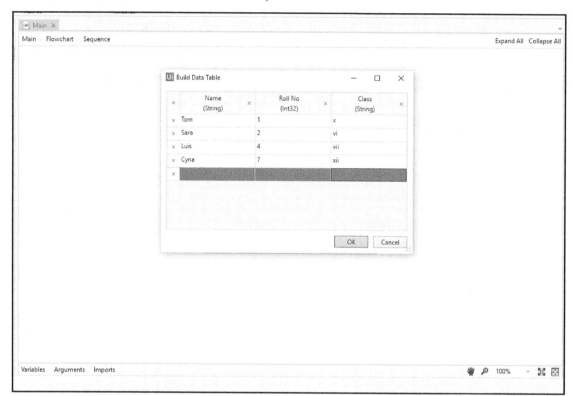

Click on the **OK** button and our data table is ready. We have to iterate over the data table's rows to make sure everything works correctly.

5. In order to store the Data Table created by **Build Data Table** activity, we have to create a data table variable MyDataTable of **DataTable** type and in order to store the result of the data table that we have dynamically built. Also, specify assign the **Output** property of the **Build Data Table** activity with this variable. Specify the data table variable's name there.

6. After our data table is ready, we will iterate the data table's rows to make sure everything works correctly. Drag and drop the **For each row** activity from the **Activities** panel inside the **Sequence** activity. Specify the data table variable's name (MyDataTable) in the expression text box of the **For each row** activity:

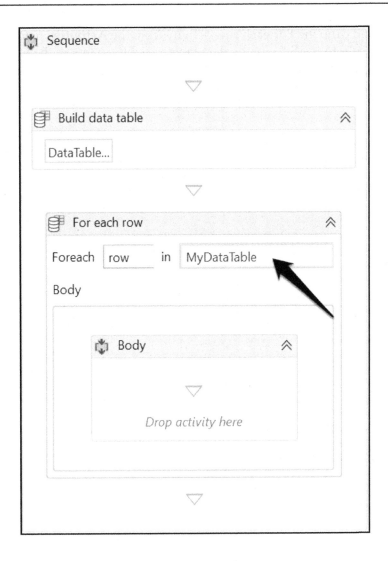

6. Drag and drop the **For each row** activity from the **Activities** panel inside the **Sequence** activity. Specify the data table variable's name in the expression text box of the **For each row** activity:

 For each and For each row are two different activities. **For each** is used to iterate over the collections, while the **For each row** activity is used to iterate over the data table rows.

7. Drag and drop a **Message box** activity inside the **For each row** activity. In
   the **Message box** activity, Inside the message box we have to write following
   string: `row("Name").ToString +"-"+ row("Roll_No").ToString + "-"+row("Class").ToString.` `row` the variable which holding data for the data
   row in each iteration:

This row variable contains all the columns of a particular row. Hence, we have to specify
which column value we want to retrieve by specifying the column name. Instead of the
column name, we can also specify the column index (the column index always starts from
zero). Hit the **Run** button to see the result.

Building a data table using data scraping (dynamically)

Using data scraping, we can build the data table at runtime. Let us consider an example of extracting data from Amazon's website. Perform the following steps:

1. Drag and drop the **Flowchart** activity from the **Activities** panel, and drag and drop the **Sequence** activity inside the **Flowchart** activity.

2. Double-click on the **Sequence** activity.

3. Drag and drop the **Open Browser** activity inside the **Sequence** activity. Specify the URL in the text box:

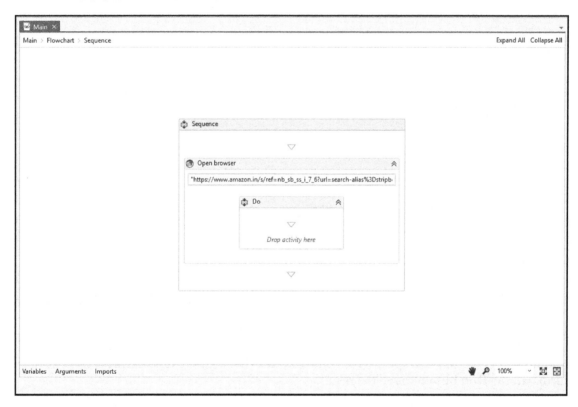

(URL: `https://www.amazon.in/s/ref=nb_sb_ss_i_7_6?url=search-alias%3Dstripbooksfield-keywords=books+for+kidssprefix=books+%2Cstripbooks%2C322crid=2OWJE9AMZYS06`)

4. Click on the **Data Scraping** icon on the top left corner of UiPath Studio. A window will pop up. Click on the **Next** button.

5. Now, there will be a pointer pointing to the UI elements of the web page. Click on the name of the book:

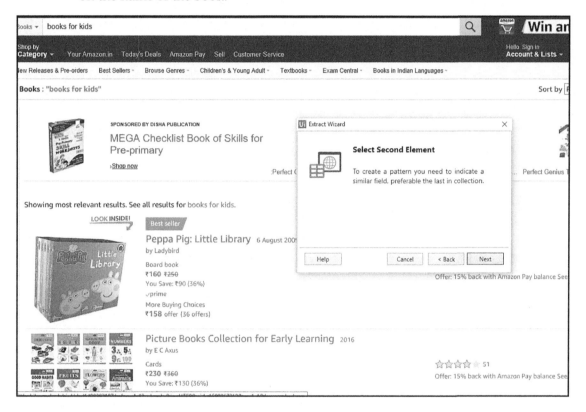

It will ask you to point to a second similar element on the web page:

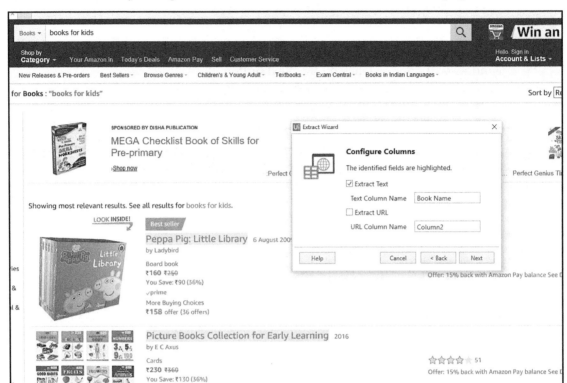

6. Point to a second similar element on that web page. Specify the name that you want to give for that extracted data column. (It will become the column name of the extracted data). Click on the **Next** button.

7. A list of names will appear in a separate window.

If you want to extract more information, then click on the **Extract correlated data** button and repeat the same process once again (just as we extracted the name of the book from Amazon's website). Otherwise, click on the **Finish** Button:

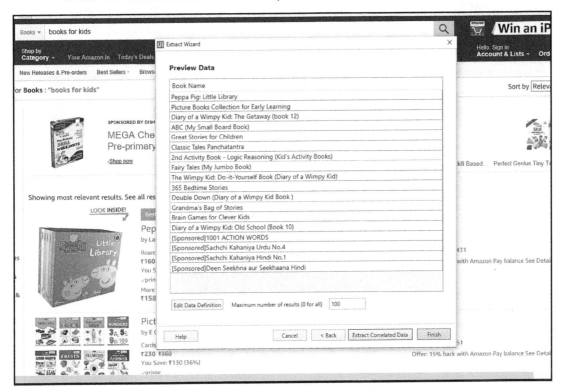

8. It will ask you to locate the next page's button/link. If you want to extract more information about the product and it spans across multiple pages, then click on the **Yes** button and point to the next page's button/link. Then, click on it. If you want to extract only the current page's data, click on the **No** button, (you can also specify the number of rows that you want to extract data from: By default it is 100):

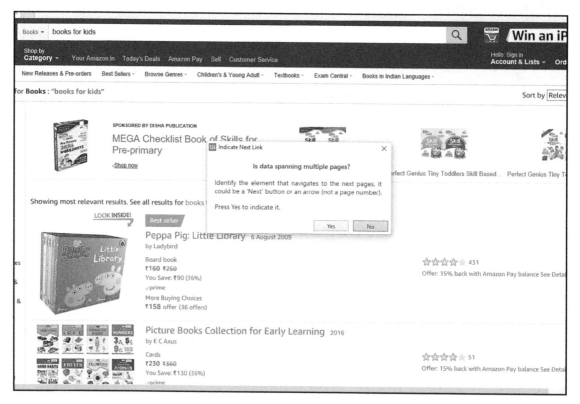

9. Data scraping generates a data table. (In this case, ExtractedDataTable is generated.) Change the scope of ExtractedDataTable to the **Flowchart** so that it is accessible within the **Flowchart** activity:

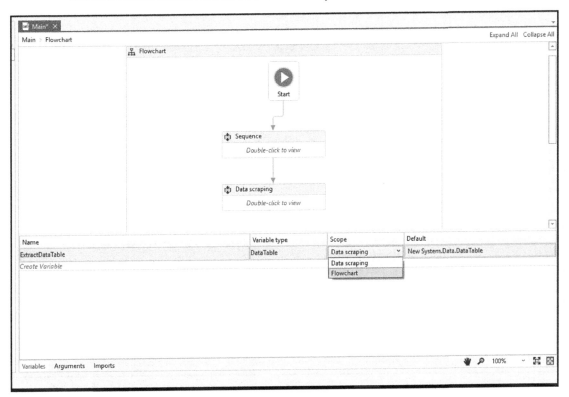

10. Drag and drop the **Output data table** activity on the **Flowchart**. Set the **Output** property of the **Output data table** activity as: ExtractedDataTable:

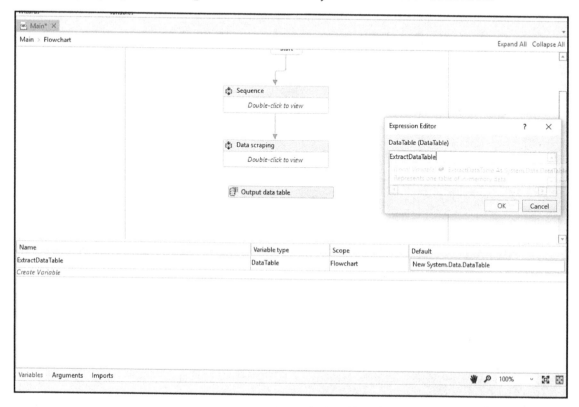

11. Connect the **Output data table** activity to the **Data Scraping** activity. Drag and drop the **Message box** activity on the Designer window. Also create a string variable to receive the text from the **Output data table** activity (in our case, we have created a `result` variable).

Specify the text property of the **Output data table** activity as the `result` variable to receive the text from the **Output data table**:

12. Connect the **Message box** activity to the **Output data table** activity. Double-click on the **Message box** and specify the text property as the `result` variable (the variable that you created to receive the text from the **Output data table** activity).

13. Hit the **Run** button and see the result.

Clipboard management

Clipboard management involves managing the activities of the clipboard, for example, getting text from the clipboard, copying selected text from the clipboard, and so on.

Let us see an example of getting text from the clipboard.

In this example, we will use Notepad. We will open Notepad, write some data into it, and then copy the data to the clipboard. We will then extract the data from the clipboard:

1. Drag and drop a **Flowchart** activity from the **Activities** panel.
2. Click on the **Recording** icon on the top of UiPath Studio. A drop-down menu will appear with the options, **Basic**, **Desktop**, **Web**, and **Citrix**, indicating the different types of recording. Select **Desktop** and click on **Record**.
3. Click on **Notepad** to open it. A Notepad window will pop up:

4. Click on the text area of Notepad. Type into the dialog box and check the empty field. (Checking the empty field will erase all existing data in Notepad before writing any new data.) Press *Enter*.

Data will be written on the Notepad text area:

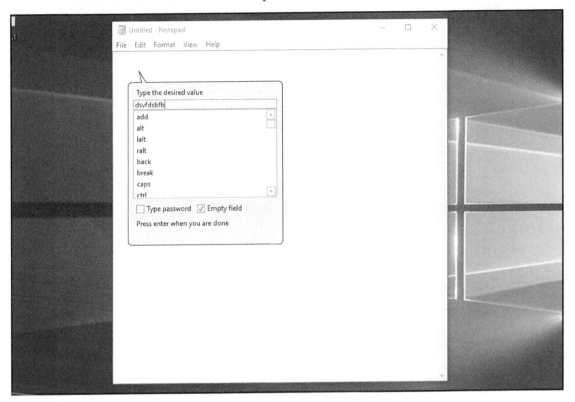

5. Click on the **Edit** button. A pop-up window will appear asking you whether you want to use an anchor. (An anchor is a relative element of the current {focused} element.) As you can see clearly, the anchor element of the **Edit** button can be the **File** or **Format** button. In this case, we have chosen the **Format** button:

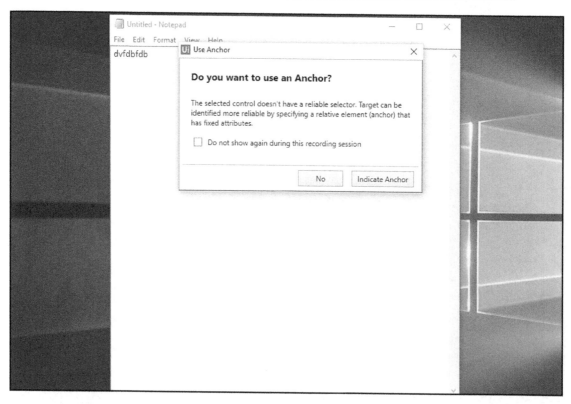

6. Then, it will automatically start recognizing the **Edit** button. Choose the **Select all** option from the drop-down list:

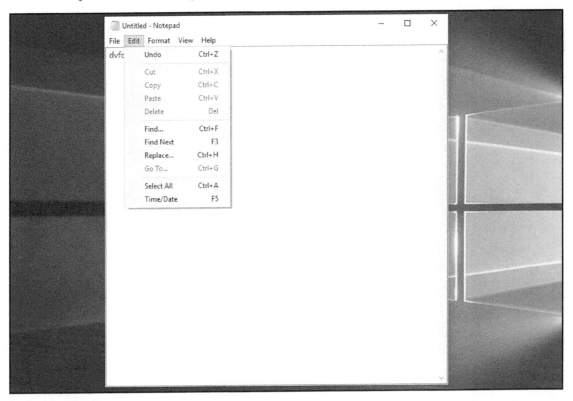

7. Once again, click on the **Edit** button. It will again ask you to indicate the anchor element. Indicate the anchor button and the **Edit** button will be highlighted, giving you a drop-down box. Select the **Copy** option:

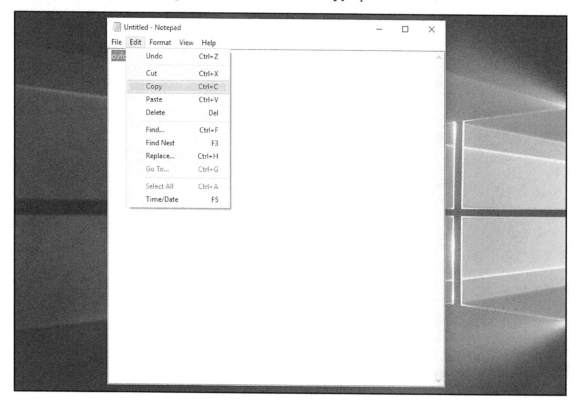

This copied text is now stored in the clipboard.

We can use the **Get from clipboard**, and **Copy selected text** activities to copy the text that is stored in the clipboard.

We will use the **Copy selected text** activity.

8. Double-click on the **Recording sequence** that is generated by the recording. Scroll down and drag and drop the **Copy selected text** and **Message box** activities inside the **Recording sequence**:

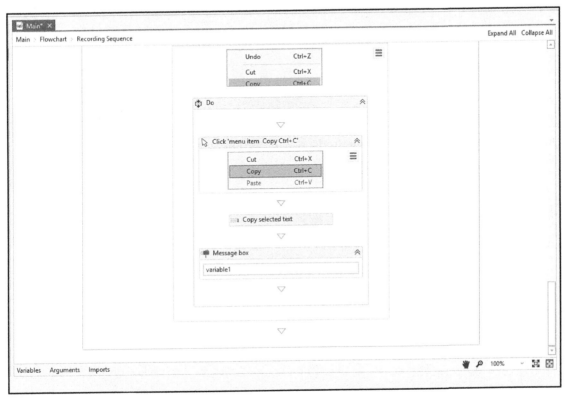

9. Create a variable of type **String** to store the output value of **Copy selected text**. This variable will receive the required text from the clipboard with the **Copy selected text** activity. Now, specify the newly created variable in the **Output** property of the **Copy selected text** activity. This will be the required selected text that we have copied into the clipboard.
10. Specify the string variable in the text property of the **Message box** activity.
11. Hit the **Run** button to see the result.

File operation with step-by-step example

In this module, we are going to operate on Excel file. The following are the methods that are frequently used with an Excel file:

- Read cell
- Write cell
- Read range
- Write range
- Append range

Once you get familiar with these methods, it will become very easy for you to use other methods too.

Read cell

This is used to read the value of a cell from an Excel file. We have a sample Excel file that we will use in this example:

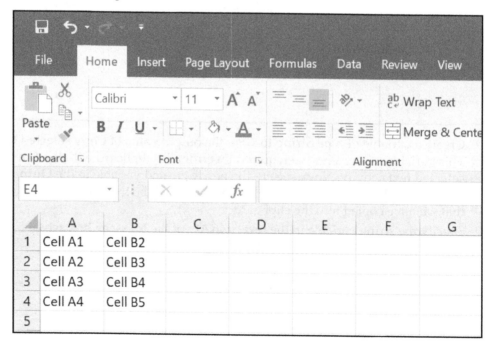

Suppose we have to read the value of the **B3** cell:

1. Drag and drop a **Flowchart** activity on the main Designer panel. Also, drag and drop an **Excel application scope** inside the **Flowchart**. Connect it to the **Start** node. Double click on Excel application scope.

> It is a good practice to use the **Excel application scope** when using Excel activities inside our project.

2. Drag and drop the **Read Cell** activity inside the **Excel application scope** activity. Specify the range value in the cell text box of the **Read Cell** activity. Create a variable of type string to hold the result produced by the **Read Cell** activity. In our case, we have created a `Result` variable. Specify the **Output** property of the **Read Cell** activity by providing the variable's name that we have created:

3. Drag and drop a **Message box** activity inside the **Excel application scope** activity and specify the string variable's name (which we created earlier) in the expression box of the **Message box** activity.

That's it. Press *F5* to see the result.

Write cell

This activity is used to write a value in a cell of an Excel file:

1. Drag and drop a **Flowchart** activity on the main Designer panel. Also, drag and drop an **Excel application scope** inside the **Flowchart** activity. Connect it to the **Start** node.
2. Drag and drop a **Write Cell** activity inside the **Excel application scope**. Specify the cell value in which we want to write in the **Range** property of the **Write Cell** activity. Also, specify the value of the **Value** property:

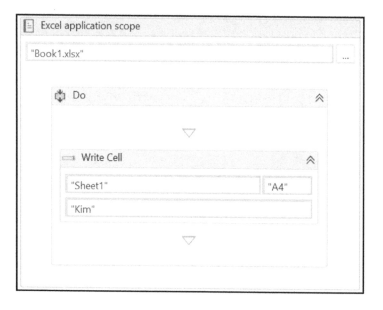

Press *F5* and see the result. Open the Excel file to see the changes:

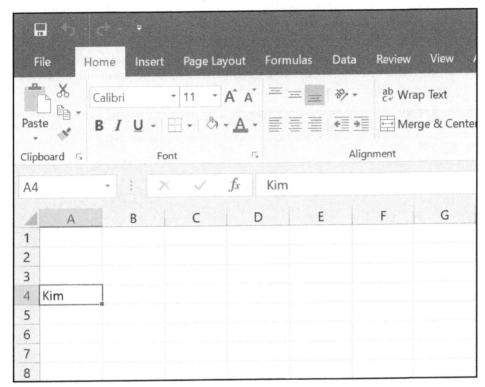

Read range

This is used to read the value up to the specified range. If the range parameter is not specified, it will read the entire Excel file:

1. Drag and drop a **Flowchart** activity on the main Designer panel. Also, drag and drop an **Excel application scope** inside the **Flowchart** activity. Connect it to the **Start** node.
2. Drag and drop a **Read Range** activity inside the **Excel application scope** activity. The **Read Range** activity produces a data table. We have to receive this data table in order to consume it. We need to create a data table variable and specify it in the **Output** property of the **Read Range** activity.

3. Drag and drop an **Output Data Table** activity inside the **Excel application scope** activity. Now, we have to specify two properties of the **Output Data Table** activity: **Data Table** property and text property. The **Data Table** property of the **Output Data Table** activity is used to convert the data table into a string format. The text property is used to supply its value in a string format. We have to receive this value in order to consume it. For this, let us create a variable of type string. Give it a meaningful name (in our case, it is **Result**):

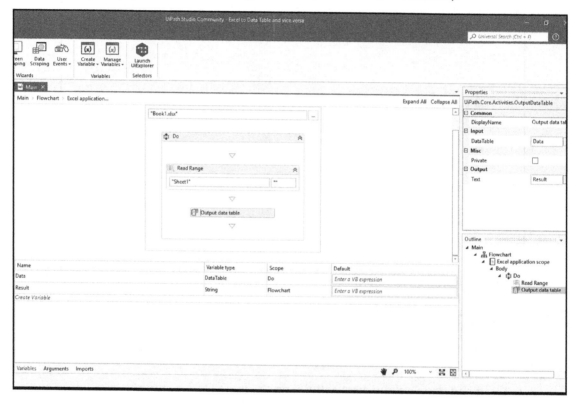

4. Drag and drop a **Message box** activity inside the **Excel application scope** activity. Also, specify the string variable's name that we created earlier inside the **Message box** activity:

That's it. Press *F5* to see the result. A window will pop up displaying your Excel file data.

Write range

This is used to write a collection of rows into the Excel sheet. It writes to the Excel file in the form of a data table. Hence, we have to supply a data table:

1. Drag and drop a **Build data table** activity from the **Activities** panel. Double-click on this activity. A window will pop up. You will notice that two columns have been generated automatically. Delete these two columns. Add your column by clicking on the + icon and specify the column name. You can also select your preferred data type. You are free to add any number of columns:

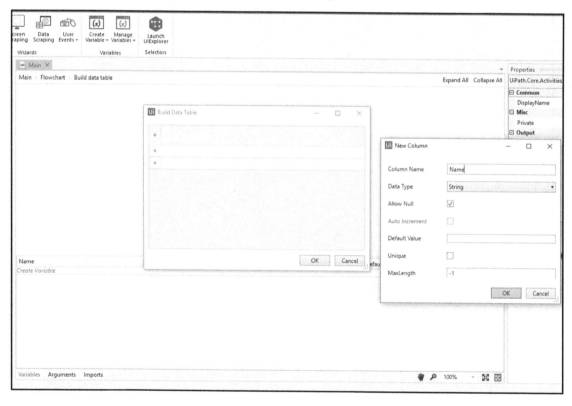

2. In this project, we are adding two columns. The procedure for adding the second column is almost the same. You just have to specify a name and its preferred data type. We have added one more column (Roll) and set the data type to **Int32** for the data table. We have also initialized this data table by providing some values in its rows.

Create a variable of type data table. Give it a meaningful name. Specify this data table name in the **Data table** property of the **Build data table** activity. We have to supply this variable in order to get the data table that we have built:

Our data table has been built successfully.

3. Drag and drop an **Excel application scope** inside the main Designer panel. You can either specify the Excel sheet path or manually select it. Connect this activity to the **Build Data Table** activity. Inside the **Excel application scope** activity, just drag and drop the **Write Range** activity:

4. Specify the data table variable name that we created earlier and set it as a **Data table** property inside the **Write Range** activity. We can also specify the range. In this case, we have assigned it as an empty string:

That's it. Hit the **Run** button or press *F5* to see the result.

Append range

This is used to add more data into an existing Excel file. The data will be appended to the end.

1. Drag and drop the **Flowchart** activity on the main Designer window. Also, drag and drop the **Excel application scope** inside the **Flowchart** activity. Connect it to the Start node.

   The **Append Range** activity requires a data table. In this program, we are going to use another sample Excel file, which has some raw data. Then, we will read this Excel file and append the data to another Excel file.

   First, we have to read its contents:

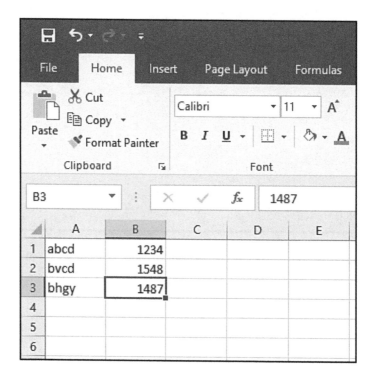

2. Drag and drop the **Read Range** activity inside the **Excel application scope**
   activity. The **Read Range** activity produces a data table. We have to receive this
   data table in order to consume it. Create a data table variable and specify it in the
   Output property of the **Read Range** activity:

3. Drag and drop the **Append Range** activity inside the **Excel application scope** activity. Specify the Excel file path in the **Append Range** activity (in which we want to append the data). Also, specify the data table (which is generated by the **Read Range** activity):

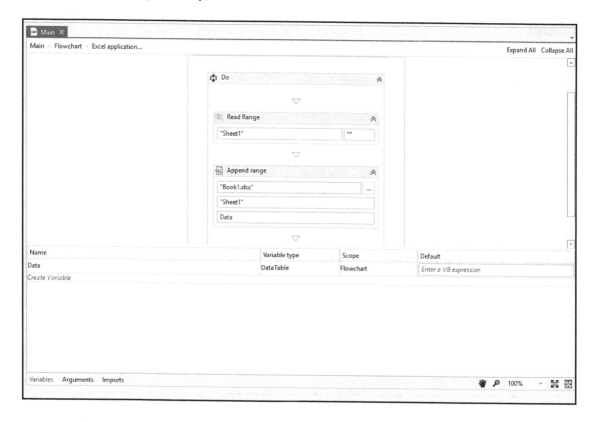

That's it. Press *F5* to see the result:

We can clearly see that the data has been appended successfully to the Excel sheet.

CSV/Excel to data table and vice versa (with a step-by-step example)

In this section, we will see how to extract data from an Excel file into a data table and vice versa. We will achieve this by:

- Reading an Excel file and creating a data table using data from the Excel file
- Creating a data table and then writing all its data to an Excel file

Reading an Excel file and creating a data table by using data from the Excel file

We have an existing Excel file and we are going to use it in our project:

1. Drag and drop the **Flowchart** activity on the main Designer window. Also, drag and drop the **Excel application scope** inside the **Flowchart**.
2. Double-click on the **Excel application scope**. You have to specify the path of your workbook/Excel file. Drag and drop the **Read Range** activity from the **Activities** panel inside the **Excel application scope**.

   The **Read Range** activity will read the entire Excel sheet. We also have the option of specifying our range. Create a variable of type data table and specify it in the **Output** property of the **Read Range** activity. This variable will receive the data table produced by the **Read Range** activity:

3. Drag and drop the **Output Data Table** activity inside the **Excel application scope** activity. Now, we have to specify two properties of the **Output Data Table** activity: the **Data Table** property and the text property. The **Data Table** property of the **Output Data Table** activity is used to convert the **Data Table** into string format.

The text property is used to supply its value in a string format. We have to receive this value in order to consume it. For this, let us create a variable of type string. Give it a meaningful name:

4. Drag and drop a **Message box** activity inside the **Excel application scope** activity. Also, specify the string variable's name that we created earlier inside the **Message box** activity.

That's it. Press *F5* to see the result. A window displaying the Excel file data will pop up.

Creating a data table and then writing all its data to an Excel file

In this project, we will build a data table dynamically and then write all its data to an Excel file:

1. Drag and drop a **Build data table** activity from the **Activities** panel. Double-click on this activity. A window will pop up. Two columns have been generated automatically; delete these two columns. Add your column by clicking on the + icon and specify the column name. You can also select your preferred data type. You are free to add any number of columns:

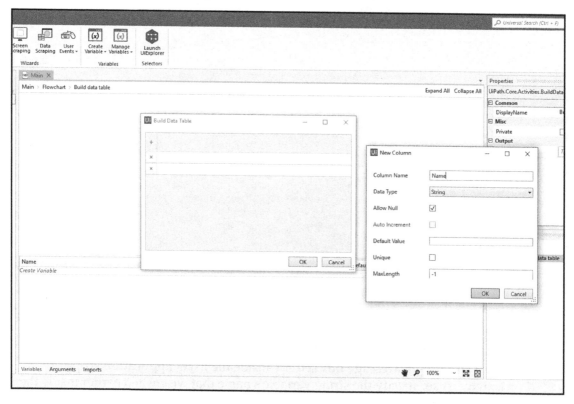

2. In this project, we are adding two columns. The procedure for adding the second column is almost the same. You just have to specify a name and its preferred data type. We have added one more column (Roll) and set the data type to **Int32** in the data table. We have also initialized this data table by giving some values to its rows.

   Create a variable of type **Data Table**. Give it a meaningful name. Specify this data table's name in the **Data Table** property of the **Build data table** activity. We have to supply this variable in order to get the data table that we have built:

Our data table has been built successfully.

3. Drag and drop the **Excel application scope** inside the main Designer window. Specify the Excel sheet's path or manually select it. Connect this activity to the **Build Data table** activity:

4. Inside the **Excel application scope** activity, drag and drop the **Write Range** activity. Specify the data table variable name that we created earlier and set it as a **Data table** property inside the **Write Range** activity. We can also specify the range. In this case, we have assigned it as an empty string:

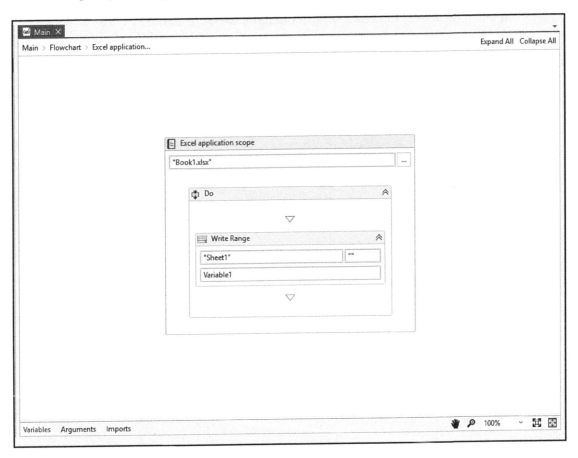

5. That's it. Hit the **Run** button or press *F5* to see the result.

Summary

In this chapter, you have learned techniques for using memory with variables. You also have learned about data tables and easy ways to manipulate data in memory.

Apart from using a variable or collection to store data, we have learned to store and manipulate data in a more persistent way using such files as CSV and Excel.

In the next chapter, we will learn to handle controls within applications in a better way.

Taking Control of the Controls

5

By now, you should be able to make fairly complex workflows and take various paths using control flows. You should now know how to store and evaluate variables to make a decision. I hope you are using a recorder extensively, as we will revisit the recorder in this chapter to learn more about it.

In this chapter, we will go into detail on how we can interact with the controls in the UI. Sometimes, you may need to click on a particular button or extract information from a textbox. Either we take some action on a control, or we read/write. We will go into detail on how to do this accurately. In this chapter, readers will learn about the various *selectors* available in UiPath to extract and take action on controls:

- Finding and attach windows
- Find controls
- Techniques to wait for a control
- Acting on controls—mouse and keyboard activities
- Working with UiExplorer
- Handling events

We will then discuss the recorder in a new context.

Extraction is a primary feature of RPA, enabling UI automation. Behind the scenes, many technologies are at work on the seamless extraction of information from the UI. When typical RPA techniques are not successful, OCR technology is used to extract information. We will learn about using OCR and other techniques in the following topics:

- Screen Scraping
- When to use OCR
- Types of OCR available
- How to use OCR

Finding and attaching windows

In this section, we are going to use the Attach Window activity.

The Attach Window activity can be found in the **Activities** panel. This activity is generally used to attach an already opened window. It is also auto-generated when we record actions using the Basic or Desktop recorder. You will get a much clearer idea after going through the example in the following section.

Implementing the Attach Window activity

In this example, we shall use the **Attach Window** activity manually. Here, we are going to attach a Notepad window and then write some text into it:

1. Create a blank project and give it a meaningful name.
2. Drag and drop a **Flowchart** activity on the Designer panel. Also, drag and drop a **Click** activity inside the Designer panel. Set this **Click** activity as the **Start** node.
3. Double-click on the **Click** activity and then click on **Indicate on screen**. Locate the Notepad icon.
4. Drag and drop the **Attach Window** activity on the main Designer panel. Connect the **Attach Window** activity to the **Click** activity.
5. Double-click on the **Attach Window** activity. Click on **Click Window on Screen** and indicate the Notepad window. The Notepad window is now attached to the previous activity:

6. For the sake of completeness, we are going to add a **Type into** activity. Just drag and drop the **Type into** activity, inside the **Attach Window** activity. Click on the **Indicate element inside window** and locate the Notepad window where you want to write the text. Write the text in the Text property of the **Type into** the activity.

7. Hit the **Run** button.

Finding the control

There are many activities which can be used to find controls on screen/ applications. These activities are used to find or wait for an UI element.

Following are the activities that help in finding the controls:

- Anchor base
- Element Exists
- Element scope
- Find children
- Find element
- Find relative element
- Get ancestor
- Indicate on screen

We will discuss all these controls one by one.

Anchor base

This control is used for locating the UI element by looking at the UI element next to it. This activity is used when we have no control over the selector. That means when we do not have a reliable selector, then we should use the **Anchor base** control to locate the UI element.

We can use the **Anchor base** control as explained in the following section:

1. Drag and drop a **Flowchart** activity on the Designer panel of a blank project. Also, drag and drop an **Anchor base** control from the **Activities** panel. Connect the **Anchor base** control with **Start**.
2. Double-click on the **Anchor base** control:

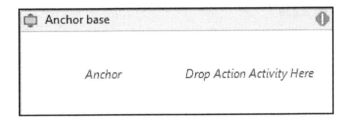

3. There are two activities that we have to supply to the **Anchor base** control: **Anchor** and action activities.
4. Drag and drop the **Anchor base** activity (for example; **Find Element** activity) in the **Anchor** field and **Action** activity (for example; **Type into**) in the **Drop Action Activity Here** field of the **Anchor base** control.

The **Anchor base** activity will find the relative element nearby the element on which you want to perform the Action, and the Action activity will perform the appropriate action that you have specified.

Element Exists

This control is used to check the availability of the UI element. It checks if the UI element Exists or not. It also returns a Boolean result if the UI Element Exists, then it returns true: otherwise, it returns false.

You can use this control to check for the UI element. In fact, it is good practice to use this control for UI elements whose availability is not confirmed or those that change frequently.

Just drag and drop the **Element Exists** control from the **Activities** panel. Double-click on it. You can see there is an **Indicate on screen** option. Click on it to indicate the UI element. It returns a Boolean result, which you can retrieve later from the Exists property. You just have to supply a Boolean variable in the **Exists** property in the **Properties** panel.

Element scope

This control is used to attach a UI element and perform multiple actions on it. You can use a bunch of actions within a single UI element.

Drag and drop the **Element scope** control and double-click on this control:

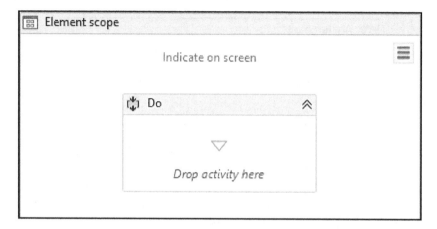

You can clearly see that you have to indicate the UI element by clicking on **Indicate on screen** and specifying all the actions that you want to perform in the **Do** sequence. You can add many activities inside the **Do** sequence.

Find children

This control is used to find all the children UI elements of a specified UI element. It also retrieves a collection of children UI elements. You can use a loop to inspect all the children UI elements or set up some filter criteria to filter out the UI elements.

Drag and drop the **Find children** control from the **Activities** panel.

Double-click on it to indicate the UI element that you want to specify. You can indicate it by clicking on **Indicate on screen**:

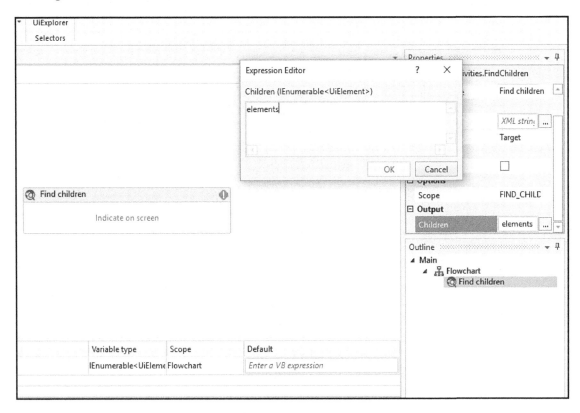

You have to supply a variable of type `IEnumerable<UIElements>` in the children property, as mentioned in the preceding screenshot. This variable is then used for retrieving the UI elements:

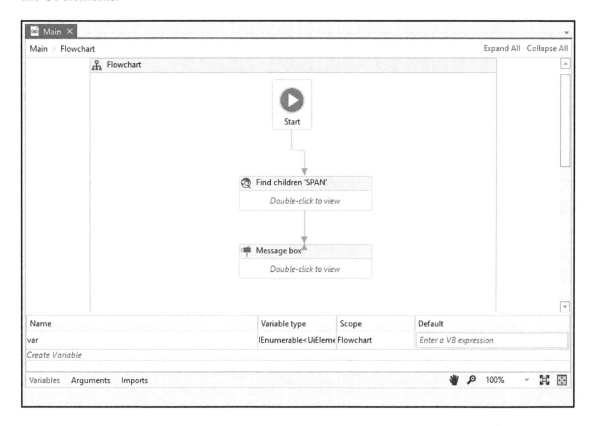

Find element

This control is used to find a particular UI element. It waits for that UI element to appear on the screen and returns it back.

You can use this control in the same way that you used the other controls. Just drag and drop this control, and indicate the UI element by clicking on **Indicate on screen**.

You can specify the variable of type UI element in the Found element property of the Find Element control to receive the UI element as output.

Find relative element

This control is similar to the Find element control. The only difference is that it uses the relative fixed UI element to recognize the UI element properly.

This control can be used in scenarios where a reliable selector is not present.

Just drag and drop this control, and indicate the UI element by clicking on **Indicate on screen**.

You can also look for its selector property after indicating the UI element for better analysis.

Get ancestor

This control is used to retrieve the ancestor of the specified UI element. You have to supply a variable to receive the ancestor element as output. You can specify the variable name in the **Ancestor** property of the **Get ancestor** control.

After receiving the ancestor element, you can retrieve its attributes, properties, and so on for further analysis:

Just drag and drop this control and indicate the UI element by clicking on **Indicate on screen**.

Indicate on screen

This control is used to indicate and select the UI element or region at runtime. It gives flexibility to indicate and select the UI element or region while running the workflow.

You just have to drag and drop this control in your project:

Do not confuse this with **Indicate on screen** written inside any activity like **Type into**. In previous examples, we have used **Indicate on screen** inside various controls (as shown in the following screenshot). This button is used to locate the region or UI element before the execution of the workflow, while the **Indicate on screen** control executes its process after the execution of the workflow:

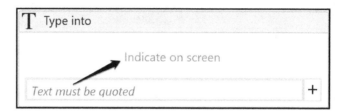

Techniques for waiting for a control

There are three techniques through which we can wait for a control. They are:

1. Wait Element Vanish
2. Wait Image Vanish
3. Wait attribute

Wait Element Vanish

This activity is used to wait for a certain element to disappear from the screen. Let us see an example where the **Wait Element Vanish** activity is in use:

1. Create a **Blank** project and give it a meaningful name.
2. Drag and drop a **Flowchart** activity on the Designer panel. Also, drag and drop the **Wait Element Vanish** activity on the Designer panel. Set this activity as the **Start** node.
3. Double-click on the **Wait Element Vanish** activity, then indicate on the screen which element needs to vanish.

Wait Image Vanish

The **Wait Image Vanish** activity is similar to the **Wait Element Vanish** activity. This activity is used to wait for an image to disappear from the UI element.

The only difference between the **Wait Element Vanish** and the **Wait Image Vanish** activities is that the former is used to wait for an element to disappear, while the latter is used to wait for an image to disappear.

Wait attribute

This activity is used to wait for the value of the specified element attribute to be equal to a string. We have to specify the string explicitly:

1. Drag and drop a **Flowchart** activity on the Designer panel. Next, drag and drop the **Wait attribute** on the Designer panel. Now, right-click on the **Wait attribute** activity and set it as the **Start** node.
2. Double-click on the **Wait attribute** activity. We have to specify three values: attribute, element, and text property. We also have to specify the element on which we have to supply the value:

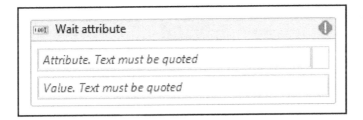

Hit the **Run** button and see the result.

Act on controls – mouse and keyboard activities

While working in UiPath Studio, we have to work with various types of controls, such as Find control, mouse control, keyboard control, and so on, to automate tasks. In this section, we are going to implement the mouse and keyboard activities.

Mouse activities

Those activities that involve interaction with the mouse fall under the category of mouse activities.

There are three mouse activities in UiPath Studio:

- Click activity
- Double-click activity
- Hover activity

The Click activity

When we have to click on a UI element on the screen, we generally use the Click activity. It is very easy to use the **Click** activity, as illustrated by the following example:

1. Drag and drop a **Flowchart** on the Designer panel. Search for mouse in the search bar of the **Activities** panel. Drag and drop the **Click** activity. Right-click on the **Click** activity and select **Set as Start Node**.
2. Double-click on the **Click** activity. Click on **Indicate on screen** and indicate the UI element you want to click on:

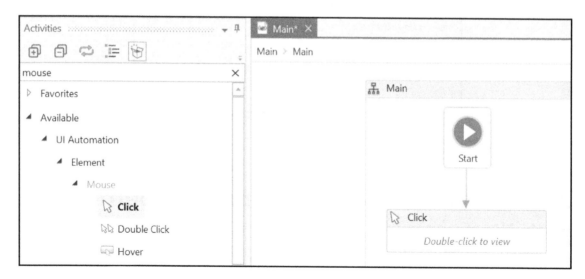

Hit the **Run** button to the see the result.

The Double-click activity

We have already seen the Click activity. The Double Click activity is similar to the Click activity. It just performs the double-click action. Using the Double click activity in your project is almost the same as click. You have to use the Double click activity instead of the Click activity and indicate the UI element, as we have done in the previous example.

The Hover activity

The **Hover** activity is used to hover over a UI element. Sometimes, we have to hover over a UI to perform an action. The Hover activity can be used in this case:

1. Drag and drop a **Flowchart** on the Designer panel. Search for mouse in the search bar of the **Activities** panel. Drag and drop the **Hover** activity. Right-click on the **Hover** activity and select **Set as Start Node**:

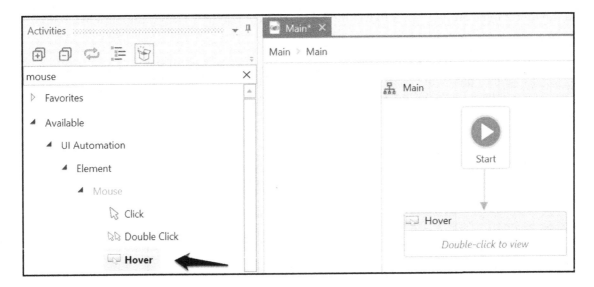

2. Double-click on the **Hover** activity. Click on **Indicate on screen** to indicate the UI element you want to hover on. That's it. We are done.

   Hit the **Run** Button to see the result.

Keyboard activities

While automating tasks, we have to deal with keyboard activities a lot of a time. Keyboard activities generally involve an interaction with a keyboard.

In UiPath Studio, the following are keyboard activities:

- Send hotkey
- Type into
- Type secure text

Send hotkey

This activity is used to send keystrokes from the keyboard as an input to the screen. Let us use an example.

In the following example, we will use the **Send hotkey** activity to scroll the Flipkart main page:

1. Drag and drop a **Flowchart** on the Designer panel. Search for Keyboard in the search bar of the **Activities** panel. Drag and drop a **Send hotkey** activity. Right-click on the **Send hotkey** activity and select **Set as Start Node**.

2. Double-click on the **Send hotkey** activity. Click on the **Indicate on screen** and indicate the required page (in our case, https://www.flipkart.com). You can assign any key by marking the checkboxes. You can also specify the key by selecting a key from the drop-down list. In our example, we have chosen the **down** key:

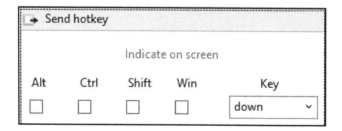

Hit the **Run** button to see the results.

To see the proper result, just scroll down the website. When this activity does its work, you will able to distinguish the change in the web page's position.

Type into activity

This activity is used to type the text into the UI element. It also supports special keys.

The **Type into** activity is quite similar to the **Send hotkey** activity. We have to send the keystrokes along with the special keys. Special keys are optional:

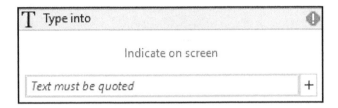

You can use this activity by simply dragging and dropping the **Type into** activity, and specifying the keystrokes and the special keys by clicking on the + icon and choosing the key from the drop-down list (if you wish to send special keys also). You also have to **Indicate on screen** the area where you want the text to be typed.

Type secure text

This activity is used to send secure text to the UI element. It sends the string in a secure way:

1. Drag and drop a **Flowchart** on the Designer panel. Search for Keyboard in the search bar of the **Activities** panel. Drag and drop the **Type secure text** activity. Right-click on the **Type secure text** activity and select **Set as Start Node**.

2. Create a variable of type **SecureString**. Now, double-click on the **Type secure text** activity and specify the variable's name in the **SecureText** property of the **Type SecureText** activity. You also have to indicate on the screen by clicking on **Indicate on screen**:

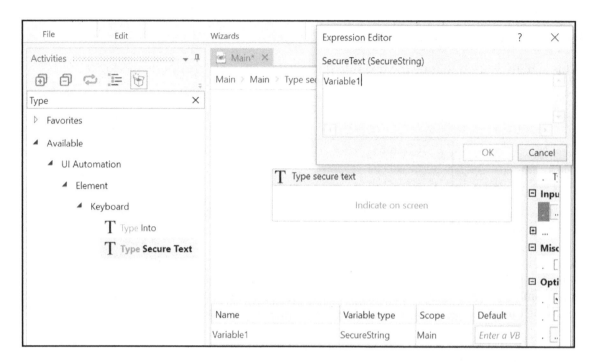

 We have not assigned a value to the `variable1` of type `SecureString`. In enterprise scenarios, you will be using the **Get credential** activity. The **Get credential** activity is used when we have to use Orchestrator. We shall learn about Orchestrator later in the book.

Working with UiExplorer

UiExplorer is a more advanced version of the selector. It is a tool that gives us the flexibility to customize the selector.

Let us try to understand the concept of UiExplorer with an example. In this example, we are going to type some text into a Notepad window. It is very easy to automate this task. You just have to use the **Type into** activity and **Indicate on screen** the area to be typed into and provide the text to be typed. Suppose you have opened a Notepad window, written some text into it, and then saved this file. If you want to write some text into it again, then UiPath Studio gives you an error.

There is nothing wrong with the implementation. What actually happens is that when you write some text in Notepad, UiPath Studio recognizes the file, app, type, title, and class, and saves this information for future recognition.

You have saved the file by providing a name. Hence, the title has been changed by the system (as the name of the Notepad window has changed). When you made the second attempt to write some text, UiPath Studio failed to recognize that instance of the Notepad window.

We can correct it by using UiExplorer. We have automated the task of writing some text in the Notepad window. Double-click on the **Type into** activity.

Click on the right side of the **Selector** property, expand **Target** property to find **Selector** property. A window will pop up. Click on the **Open in UiExplorer** button:

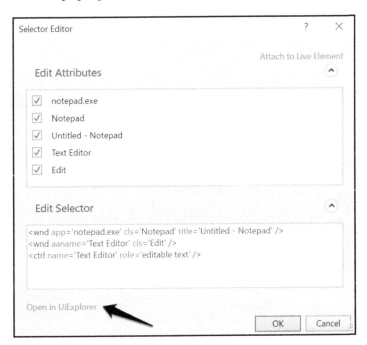

A window will pop up. You can see the **Selector Editor** window. Analyze all the text written there. You will notice the title: **Untitled-Notepad**.

You just have to edit this title. Just specify **test-Notepad** between the quotes:

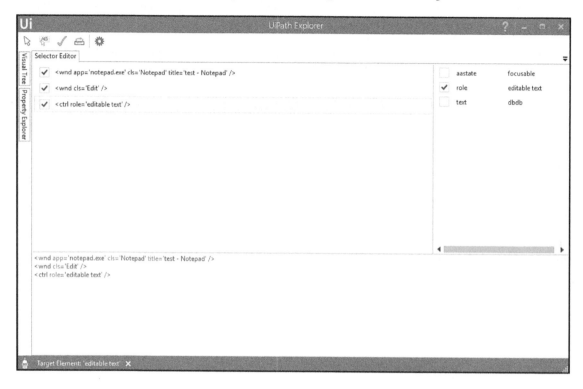

The problem was when you opened the Notepad window, UiPath Studio saved the title attribute as **Untitled-Notepad**. You saved the file and its title changed to **test-Notepad**. When you tried to write some text next time, it did not recognize the title as it had been changed from **Untitled-Notepad** to **test-Notepad**.

You just have to edit the title attribute to remove the error.

 UiExplorer is used to customize the selector and to view attributes and their associated values. View it carefully and inspect the attribute that should be changed.

Handling events

An event occurs when some action is performed. There are different types of events:

- Element triggering event
- Image triggering event
- System triggering event

Element triggering events

This type of event deals with clicking and keypress events.

Click trigger

This event occurs when a specified UI element is clicked.

Before using the Click trigger, we have to use the **Monitor events** activity. Without **Monitor events**, the Click trigger cannot be used.

Double-click on **Monitor events**. Drag and drop the Click trigger inside **Monitor events**. Also, drag and drop the activity in the **Event handler** section of **Monitor events**. In this case, we have used the **Message box** activity and also specified the string value.

Inside the Click trigger, you have to indicate the UI element that you want to click on:

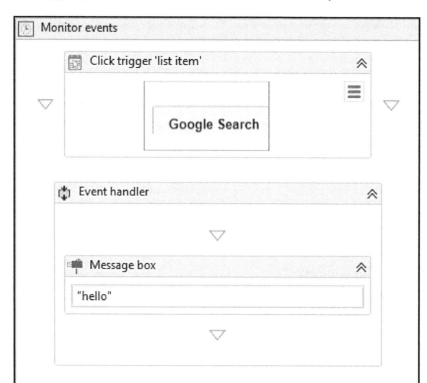

When the Click action is performed on the specified button, then the event handler will be called and the activities inside the event handler will be executed.

Key press trigger

This event is similar to the Click trigger. A Key press trigger event occurs when keystrokes have been performed on some particular UI element. It calls the **Event handler** when it is triggered.

While using **Key press trigger** event you have to specify the key or combination of keys.

Indicate the UI element on which you want to perform the action:

When the keys are pressed on the specified UI element, the event handler will be called.

Image triggering events

The Click image trigger is an image tiriggering event.

Click image trigger, as the name suggests, is used for when we click an image. You just have to use the Click image trigger event inside the Monitor event and indicate the image. Upon clicking the indicted image in the Click image trigger event, the event handler will be called.

System triggering events

The following are System triggering events:

- Hotkey trigger
- Mouse trigger
- System trigger

Hotkey trigger

This event is raised when special keys are pressed. As we have already looked at triggering events, you can use the Hotkey trigger event on your own. You have to use this event inside the Monitor event.

Specify the special key or combination of keys. Also, provide the event handler that will be called when the event occurs.

Mouse trigger

This event is fired when the mouse button is pressed. Use this event inside the Monitor event and specify the Mouse button: Either the left mouse button, middle mouse button, or the right mouse button.

System trigger

This event is used when you have to use all of the keyboard events, all of the mouse events, or both.

In the following screenshot, we have dragged and dropped the **System trigger** event into **Monitor events**. You can specify the trigger input property:

Revisit recorder

You have already learned about Task recording in `Chapter 2`, *Record and Play*. In this section, we will explore recording a bit more.

As we discussed earlier, there are four types of recording in UiPath Studio:

- Basic recording
- Desktop recording
- Web recording
- Citrix recording

Basic recording

This is used to record the actions of applications that have a single window. Basic Recording uses a full Selector. It works better for applications performing a single action. It is not suitable for applications with multiple windows.

There are two types of selectors, partial selectors and full selectors. A Full selector has all the attribute to recognize a control or application. The Basic recording uses full selectors.

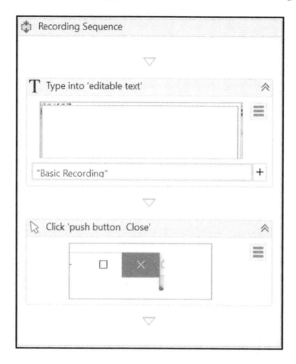

Please note that, in the preceding image that there are different activities but those activities are not wrapped inside containers, it is generated by Basic recorder. Basic recording generates different activities and places them directly in the sequence with full selector.

You have already seen how to automate tasks using the Basic recorder; now, let us cover other recorders.

Desktop recording

This is similar to Basic recording with the added advantage of working with multiple actions. It is most suitable for automating Desktop applications.

Desktop recorder generates Partial selectors. The Partial selectors, have a hierarchical structure. They are split into parent child views for recognizing the UI element properly.

Please note in the preceding image there is a **Attach Window** activities and other activities are nested under it. This flow is generated **Desktop** recorder:

Web recording

Web Recording can be done by using the Web recorder. For recording web actions, the UiPath extension for that browser should be installed. Otherwise, you will not able to automate tasks or actions using Web recording.

You just have to click on the Setup icon and then click on Setup Extensions. Now, choose your browser and click on it. The UiPath extension will be added to your specified browser.

Web Recording is similar to Desktop Recording. You just have to record the actions and save it.

Create a **Blank** project. Drag and drop a **Flowchart** activity. Now, click on the **Recording** icon and choose **Web** recording. You can record your actions on the web on your own and then save it. In our case, we have opened a web page using Google Chrome and logged in to http://www.google.com. Then, we started the recording by clicking on the Record button of the web recorder. Next, we typed some text in the search bar of Google and performed the Click activity. Then, we pressed the *Esc* key to exit the recording and clicked on the **Save and Exit** button. Now, a recording sequence is generated in our Designer panel. Connect this sequence to the **Start** node. Hit the **Run** button to see the result. In the following screenshot, you can see the sequence generated by the Web recorder:

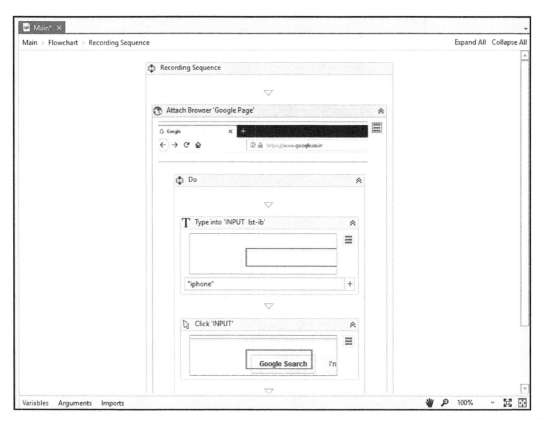

Before running the UiPath workflow, make sure you are on the Google homepage.

We have seen Web recording and it is very easy. There is also another option to extract information from websites.

We can easily extract information from websites using data scraping.

Suppose we want to extract data from Amazon's website. Say we want to search for books on Amazon and extract the search results. Extracting data from websites becomes very easy with data scraping:

1. Create a blank project and give it a meaningful name. Click **Create**.
2. Log on to Amazon's website and search for books. A detailed list of books is listed on your screen:

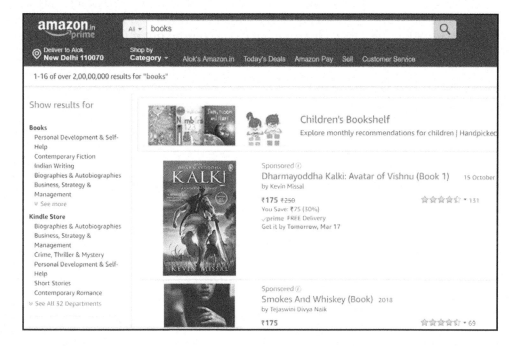

3. Drag and drop a **Flowchart** activity on the Designer panel. Now, click on the **Data Scraping** icon. A window will pop up.
4. Click on the **Next** button.
5. You have to indicate the first book's entities. Entities can be name, price, author, and so on. It is your choice.
6. Lets's, indicate the book's name. After that, it will ask for the next book's entities. Indicate the second book entity as well. Click on **Next**.

7. This means you have to indicate the second book's entities: however, the entities will be the same. If you choose name as the first book's entity then you have to be specific and choose name as the second book's entity. You should not choose name as the first book's entity and then choose price as the second book's entity.

8. Again, a window will pop up asking you to configure the columns. You can also extract the URL. If you want to do this, check the **Extract URL** checkbox.

9. You can specify the column name as well. Click on the **Next** button.

10. As you can see, all the book names are extracted to a window. If you want to extract more columns or more entities, then click on **Extract Correlated Data** and you have to again indicate another entity of the book to extract more columns, as we have done previously. After that, all the data will be extracted and will be added to this table. Here, we have one column but if you extract more entities, then more columns will be added to this table:

11. Click on the **Finish** button. If the results of your query span multiple pages, it will ask you to indicate the page navigation link on the website (Next button of the website that we used to navigate to another/next page). If the results of your query span multiple pages, click on the **Yes** button and indicate the link, otherwise click on the **No** button.

12. We have clicked on the **No** button. A data scraping sequence is generated in our **Flowchart**.

    It will also generate a data table. You can retrieve the information from the data table.

Citrix

When dealing with the Remote Desktop connection, methods such as Basic Recording and Desktop Recording cannot be used. In an RDP environment, images will be sent from one desktop to another, and will be mapped by analyzing the position of the pointer of the mouse button. Hence, basic and desktop recording cannot be used, as these recording techniques fail to interact with the images. In a Citrix environment, we have the **Click Text** and **Click Image** activities, using which we can work with images with ease.

You can clearly see the activities that are listed in a Citrix Recording:

1. Click Image
2. Click Text
3. Type
4. Select & Copy
5. Screen Scraping
6. Element
7. Text
8. Image

All these activities are used extensively in a Citrix environment.

You can use these activities as you have used Basic Recording or Desktop Recording: the only difference is that you have to indicate a point on the screen, or you have to indicate an anchor element as you have used in previous sections.

Screen Scraping

Screen Scraping is a method of extracting data from documents, websites, and PDFs. It is a very powerful method for extracting text. We can extract text using the Screen Scraper wizard. The Screen Scraper wizard has three scraping methods:

- Full Text
- Native
- OCR

We shall elaborate on each of these methods one by one. One should have a clear understanding of these methods in order to know when to use which method. There will be situations when we have to choose the best method for our needs:

- **Full text**: The Full text activity is used to extract information from various types of documents and websites. It has a 100% accuracy rate. It is the fastest method among all three methods. It even works in the background. It is also capable of extracting hidden text. However, it is not suitable for Citrix environments.
- **Native**: This is similar to the Full text method but has some differences. It has a slower speed than the Full text method. It has a 100% accuracy rate, like the Full text method. It does not work in the background. It has an advantage over the Full text method in that it is also capable of extracting the text's position. It cannot extract hidden text. It also does not work with a Citrix environment.
- **OCR**: This method is used when the previous two methods fail to extract information. It uses the two OCR engines: Microsoft OCR and Google OCR. It has also a scale property: you can choose the scale level as per your need. Changing the scale property will give the best results:

Capability Method	Speed	Accuracy	Background Execution	Extract text position	Extract hidden text	Support for Citrix
Full Text	10/10	100%	Yes	No	Yes	No
Native	8/10	100%	No	Yes	No	No
OCR	3/10	98%	No	Yes	No	Yes

Let us consider an example of extracting text from the UiPath website's main page:

1. Create a **Blank** project and give it a meaningful name.
2. Log on to the UiPath website by logging in to `https://www.uipath.com/` in your browser.
3. Drag and drop a **Flowchart** activity on the Designer panel. Click on the **Screen Scraping** icon and locate the area from which you want to extract the information. Just choose an area on the UiPath website. A window will pop up stating that the **AUTOMATIC method failed to scrape this UI Element**.

   By default, the **Screen Scraper Wizard** chooses the best scraping method to extract data, but it failed to do so in our case:

4. Try choosing another method. We shall choose the Full text method. This too will fail. Next, choose the Native method. This will also fail, as you can see in the following screenshot:

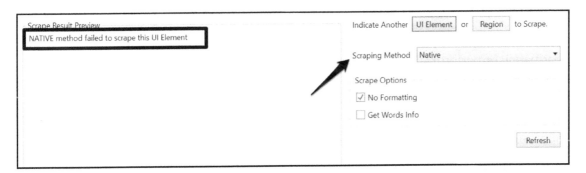

5. This time, choose the OCR Scraping method. You can clearly see the extracted text:

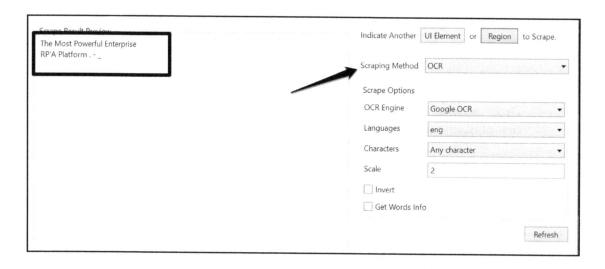

When to use OCR

There are some scenarios where normal activities such as **Get Text** and **Click Text** activities fail to extract the text or perform an action. This is when OCR comes in, giving us the flexibility to perform actions when existing activities fail to do their job.

OCR stands for Optical Character Recognition. It is a text recognition technique that transforms printed documents that are scanned into electronic formats.

OCR is used mainly for images, scanned documents, PDFs, and so on, to extract information or perform actions. Extracting information or data from images, scanned documents, or PDFs is a very tedious job. Normal activities are not recommended for extracting these types of inputs. OCR uses a different method and approach to extract the information.

There are two OCRs available in UiPath Studio:

1. Microsoft OCR
2. Google OCR

Microsoft's OCR is known as MODI, and Google's OCR is called Tesseract. OCR is not limited to only these two types of OCR. You are free to use another type of OCR.

Consider we are going to extract some text from a Word document by using the **Get Text** activity:

1. Create a **Blank** project and give it a meaningful name.
2. Drag and drop a **Flowchart** activity on the Designer panel. Also, drag and drop a **Get Text** activity inside the Designer panel. Now right-click on the **Get Text** activity and choose **Set as Start Node**.
3. Double-click on the **Get Text** activity. Click on **Indicate on screen**. Now indicate the text from which you want to extract information. You have to supply the output value for receiving the text from the **Get text** activity. Create a **GenericValue** type of variable and specify the variable name `str`.
4. Drag and drop a **Message box** activity. Connect it to the **Get Text** activity. Double-click on the **Message box** activity and specify the variable's name (str) that you created earlier:

Hit the **Run** button to see the result. You can clearly see in this example that using the **Get Text** activity does not extract, text properly.

This is where OCR enters the picture. In the next section, we will see the extraction of text using OCR.

Types of OCR available

There are two OCRs available in our UiPath Studio:

1. Microsoft OCR
2. Google OCR

However, we are free to import other OCR engines into our project.

Both the Microsoft and Google OCR engines have their own advantages and disadvantages. The advantages of Google OCR include the following:

- Multiple language support can be added in Google OCR
- Suitable for extracting the text from a small area
- It has full support for color inversion
- It can filter only allowed characters

The advantages of Microsoft OCR include the following:

- Multiple languages are supported by default
- It is suitable for extracting text from a large area

OCR is not 100% accurate. It is useful for extracting text that other methods cannot successfully do. It works with all applications, including Citrix.

Microsoft and Google's OCRs are not the optimum for every situation. Sometimes, we have to look for more advanced OCRs to recognize more sophisticated text, such as handwritten documents and so on.

There is another OCR available in UiPath Studio, known as the Abbyy OCR Engine. You can find this OCR engine in the **Activities** panel by searching for OCR.

If you cannot find this OCR listed in the **Activities** panel, you need to install the UiPath.Core.Activities package:

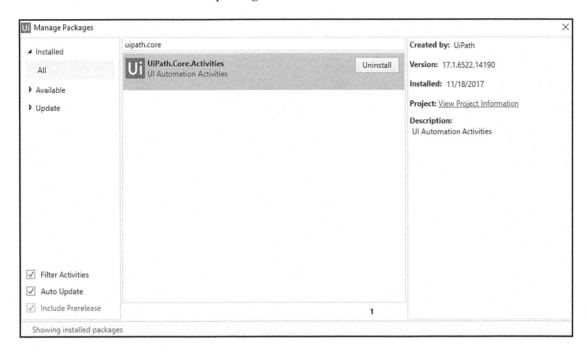

In the previous screenshot, the package has already been installed, which is why there is an **Uninstall** button on the right-hand side of UiPath.Core.Activities.

How to use OCR

In this section, we are going to see how we can use OCR. Suppose we have an image and we have to extract the text in it. In such a scenario, OCR becomes very handy.

In the following example, we are going to use a random Google image with some text in it, as follows:

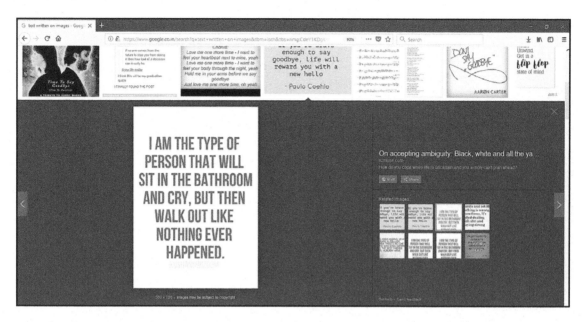

To extract text from the previous image, perform the following steps:

1. Open UiPath Studio and click on a **Blank** project. Give it a meaningful name. On the Designer panel, drag and drop a **Flowchart** activity.
2. Next, drag and drop a **Get OCR Text** activity from the **Activities** panel and set it as the start node. Double-click on it and click on the **Indicate on screen** option. Choose the specific area from which you want to extract the text from the image. In our case, we are using an image that we have searched for on Google.

3. Now, click on the **Text** property of the **Get OCR Text** activity. A window will pop up as shown in the following screenshot. Right-click inside the window and choose **Create Variable**. Give it a meaningful name, press *Enter*, and click on the **OK** button. A variable will be created with that name:

5. Drag and drop the **Message box** activity. Connect it to the Get OCR with text activity. Double-click on the **Message box** activity and specify the variable name that you have created earlier in the expression box. (In our case, it is the `result` variable).

Press *F5* to see the result.

Try to change the scale property of the OCR engine. It will give you better results in some cases.

Avoiding typical failure points

There are many scenarios where the normal implementation would fail. We are going to discuss these failure points and will see how to tackle them.

In this section, we will work with the following entities to tackle failure points:

- Selectors
- Scope of the variable
- Delay
- Element Exists
- Try / Catch
- toString method

Selectors

Sometimes, it is tedious to deal with selectors while working with them. This is because a selector has attributes, title, and class properties. When we select a UI element using the selector, it stores all these properties. Different instances of an application may have different properties of a UI element.

The problem with selectors is when you select a UI element, it captures its properties. These properties will differ when we select the UI element of a different instance of an application with the selector. Hence, the property will differ and the selector will fail to recognize the same UI element of another instance of the application.

We can easily fix this problem by using wildcard characters or by attaching it to a live element. Two wildcard characters are available with UiPath:

1. The question mark symbol, ?, which replaces one character
2. The asterisk symbol, that is, *, which replaces a number of characters

We have to simply replace the variables (the name that changes continuously) with wildcard characters.

We can also use the **Attach to live element** option from the selector property window and indicate the element again. It automatically detects the variable properties and fixes them for us.

Scope of the variable

Sometimes we create a variable inside a Sequence or Do activity. In doing so, the scope of the variable is limited to only that activity.

When we try to access a variable from outside its scope, it cannot be accessed. We have to change the scope of the variable.

Delay activity

In some situations, we have to wait for a particular action. For example, when opening the Outlook application, it needs to connect to the server (for synchronization). When it is opened, it takes some time (the UI element is not stable at this stage).

In the meantime, the robot's activity is waiting for the UI element to be stable so that it can perform the action. After waiting for some time, if the UI element is not stable, it results in an error because the activity cannot find the UI element. Thus, we have to add a Delay activity to ensure that the UI element is stable for action. Specify the time for the delay in the expression text box of the Delay activity. This activity will delay the process for the specified period of time.

Element Exists

This activity is used to ensure that the required Element Exists. It is used to ensure that the element we are looking for exists in this context.

This is a good way of checking whether the activity exists or not.

Try/Catch

This is an exception handling mechanism used to tackle exceptions.

Put all suspicious activities inside the `Try` block. If an error occurs, it can be detected by the `Catch` block.

toString

Sometimes, we forget to use the `toString` method with variables and we end up with an error.

For example, when outputting an integer variable inside the **Message box**, we have to apply the `toString` method.

Summary

In this chapter, we learned about the various types of controls available in UiPath, including types of mouse and keyboard activities. We also revisited the Recording feature of UiPath Studio, this time learning more advanced features. UiExplorer is another topic we forayed into, which is basically used to customize the selector. Furthermore, we learned about OCR, its types, and its uses. Finally, we dealt with the extraction of data using Screen Scraping.

6

Tame that Application with Plugins and Extensions

So far, you have learned how to record steps to automate and also learn about control flow, and the use of variables and data tables. The most important part was understanding and mastering controls. Unless you are able to identify controls of an application properly, it is not possible to successfully automate a process. Now, in this chapter, we will step up to learn how to use external plugins and extensions. UiPath has many plugins and extensions to ease UI automation, apart from basic extraction and interaction with the desktop screen. These plugins allow us to directly interact with those applications or ease UI automation. Some of the important sections that are going to be covered in this chapter are:

- Terminal plugin
- SAP Automation
- Java plugin
- Citrix Automation
- Mail plugin
- PDF plugin
- Web integration
- Excel and Word plugins
- Credentials management
- Extensions: Java, Chrome, Firefox, and Silverlight

Terminal plugin

The Terminal plugin is used to execute commands in textual format (generally a black window). It works faster than the **Graphical User Interface (GUI)** methodology. It also has a broader scope in terms of authority and permissions.

In UiPath Studio, there is a NuGet Package called `UiPath.Terminal.Activities`. Terminal activity is pre-installed in UiPath Studio. In case it is not installed, we have to install it manually. To check whether the Terminal activity is installed or not, simply search for `Terminal` in the **Activities** panel. It will list all the terminal activities. If no activities are listed in the **Activities** panel, you have to install the `UiPath.Terminal.Activities` package.

To install Terminal activity NuGet Package, click on the **Manage Package** icon, as shown in the following screenshot:

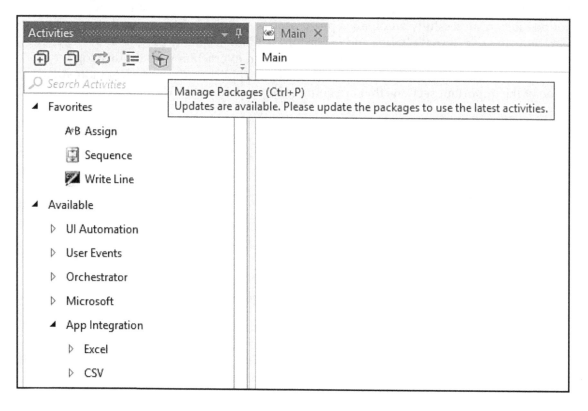

The Manage Packages window will appear. Search for `terminal` in the search bar. As shown in the following screenshot, there is an **Uninstall** button next to **UiPath.Terminal.Activities**. This is because the **Terminal** activity is already installed in UiPath Studio. If it is not installed, an **Install** button will appear next to the **UiPath.Terminal.Activities**:

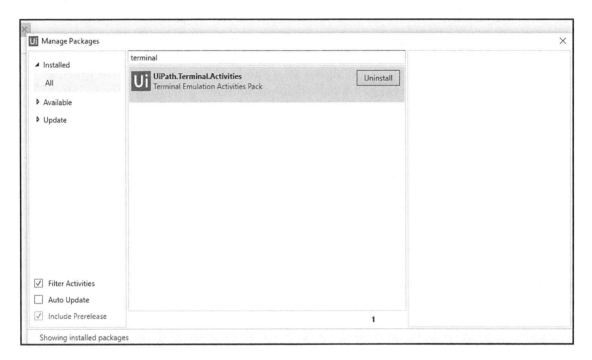

SAP automation

Whether in software or in the form of mechanical Robots, automation is everywhere. Businesses have not only the latest information but the most accurate too. In today's market, if businesses cannot be kept up to date then they will suffer.

SAP automation with UiPath is integrated with the latest techniques that are more suitable for organizations. Today, SAP automation is becoming the buzzword in the IT industry. These days, error-prone databases and unfilled/partially filled documents are mostly discarded.

With SAP automation from UiPath Studio, these can be easily avoided. It automates tasks easily and makes organizations more productive.

Some of the advantages of UiPath's SAP Automation are listed as follows:

1. It is compatible with all the SAP automation techniques that are best suited to the organization.
2. It is accurate (99.999 % of the time) and delivers the best results. It avoids typical errors that humans/employees would be likely to make.
3. Human employees demand higher salary and consideration has to be given to (**full-time employees**) FTE too. SAP automation has a modular approach to FTE.
4. It is scalable. Just set it up with hundreds of Robots and you do not have to monitor them. There is no need to constantly watch them. The Robots can work independently.

SAP Automation requires some steps with which you should be careful while automating. There are some situations when the Click activity fails to recognize the UI element. Click Text activity and Click Image activity are used when Click activity does not work in some situations while automating SAP.

There are some scenarios when we have to extract tabular data from SAP. Iterating through the table is not easy. In such case use selectors to recognize the table cell. You can implement a loop to iterate through each table cell. Now, how will you know when your loop should stop iterating the table cell? You can put your code inside a Try Catch activity and when an exception occurs (exception occurs when the loop encounters an empty table cell or when the end of the table has been reached), it is caught by the Catch block. In this way, you will be able to iterate through all the table cells.

While interacting with checkboxes and radio buttons, make use of Get attribute activity to check whether they are checked or not.

When dealing with elusive UI elements, for example, a small button to the right of some text, you have to think in terms of human actions. How would a human react to such steps?

How SAP Automation affects data entry jobs

Data entry is a complex task. Employees have to work in a smart manner during the entire process, constantly checking for errors. There are some tasks that employees/humans do well, such as scanning a form for some information and extracting it. They can categorize the documents properly. Tasks like these are considered to be difficult for a system/computer. Of course, employees/humans can make errors that no software ever would. UiPath takes the best of both worlds—the benefits of automation and the benefits of mimicking humans, making software Robots that can be trained to scan forms, copy data, or notice a key being pressed. This also significantly reduces errors in the programs (in comparison to human employees undertaking the same tasks).

In addition to these processes, UiPath uses a method to ignore unrelated information on a website, SAP software, or any other application, only giving priority to the important ones.

It means that no matter how much your SAP application is difficult to handle, UiPath handles every action with ease. It can scale with any application on any platform.

Examples where SAP automation is used commonly

Some examples in which SAP automation is used are:

1. Filling in a form from any application.
2. Copying and pasting data between SAP and other applications.
3. Comparing data fields on the screen.
4. Updating the status of an entity in a system.
5. Scraping data from any application/websites.

UiPath is simple to use. In fact, there is no need to know a programming language or any scripting language. UiPath's Robots can be trained by the visual programming interface. You can define a complex workflow for your existing application and train your Robot. Once trained, Robots can run independently at a lower cost. It is estimated that a software Robot's work efficiency is equal to three employees. It saves a lot of time and money.

UiPath Studio comes with built-in libraries and activities so that the Robot can be trained and processes can be automated. It means that it can copy and paste the entities from one application to the other so that employees have more time to do complex logical work. It increases productivity and efficiency.

Java plugin

The Java plugin software is a component of the **Java Runtime Environment (JRE)**. The JRE allows applets (software programs written in the Java programming language) to run in various browsers.

Why are we using the Java plugin with UiPath Studio?

Suppose we have to automate a Java application. We cannot use pre-installed activities with the Java application as it will not recognize them properly. Hence, in order to use activities with the Java application, we have to install the Java plugin.

Follow these steps to install the Java plugin inside UiPath Studio:

1. Click on the **SETUP** wizard:

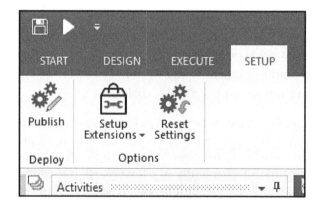

2. Next, click on **Setup Extensions** and choose **Java**:

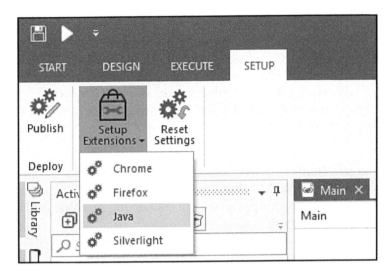

A confirmation window will pop up stating that the Java plugin has been installed successfully.

To check whether the Java plugin is working properly, open UiExplorer, click on any Java application, and select an element. If the entire window is selected instead of that element, then your Java plugin has not been installed successfully. On the other hand, if the element is selected properly, then your Java plugin has been installed successfully.

Citrix automation

We have previously dealt with common automations—automating desktop applications or web applications. It is easy when we deal with these applications having graphical user interfaces. UiPath identifies the elements that we have clicked on and recognizes them. Thus, the next time the Robot executes a process, it successfully identifies the same element. We have already seen these types of action.

But what if we have a remote desktop connection and we need to automate an application using this remote desktop connection? It will be a tedious job.

Can we automate an application running on another machine while we are accessing it remotely with the activities that we have used with simple GUI? The answer is no.

Let's investigate why this is so. Suppose we have to automate a desktop application so that the Robot does all the necessary actions on that application. We can simply use the click, double-click, and other activities to automate it. We cannot, however, use these activities when establishing a connection with another system remotely. Why do normal activities such as click and double click not work with a remote desktop connection? The problem with a remote desktop connection is that it sends the images of a system to another system. Recording activities such as click or double click may not accurately capture the position of that control inside the remote system.

You will get a better understanding with this example. Consider that machine A has a screen whose resolution is 1366×768, while another machine B has a screen whose resolution is 1024×768 resolution. Suppose we are connecting machine A to machine B using a remote desktop connection.

Now machine B with a resolution of 1024×768 is being accessed by machine A. What actually happens is that the frontend image of the machine B window is being sent to machine A. Hence, we cannot click on an image.

Since both machines have different resolutions, sending the coordinates of an element to another machine is error-prone or difficult during the remote desktop connection.

We have pointed out two problems when automating through the remote desktop connection:

1. We cannot click on an image
2. Sending the coordinates of an element to another machine is error-prone

You will be wondering how we can overcome these two problems. Well, UiPath Studio comes with an environment called Citrix. Using the Citrix environment, it becomes very easy for us to automate an application when accessing it remotely.

It has a lot of options so that clicking on an image or sending the coordinates of an element become easy.

Some activities that Citrix supports are:

1. Click Image
2. Click text
3. Type
4. Send hotkey
5. Select and Copy

6. Screen Scraping and Scrape Data
7. Copy text

To automate using the Citrix environment, we have to select the Citrix Recording mode. In UiPath Studio, click on **Recording** and select **Citrix**:

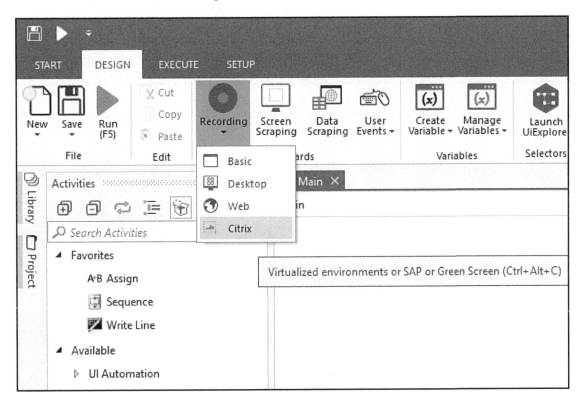

Now, you can use a variety of controls and activities that help in automate applications remotely.

How does the Citrix environment work?

Citrix gives us the flexibility to work in **Remote Desktop Protocol** (**RDP**). It captures the image and its position along with its relative elements so that they can easily be identified on another machine. No matter what the resolution of the screen, it can recognize elements easily. Have a look:

(We are not going to use RDP here. This is an example just to demonstrate the activity of Citrix).

Suppose we have to type into the Google search bar and click on the **Search** button.

Click on the **Recording** icon at the top of UiPath Studio. Select the **Citrix** option. A window will pop up. Now navigate to **Google** and click on the **Type** activity from the pop-up menu:

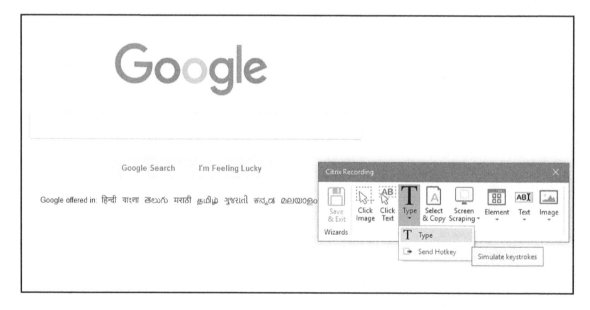

A pop-up window will be shown. Just type the text that you want to search for. Also, check the **Empty Field** option. Press **Enter**:

It will again show you a pop-up window. Now select **Click Image** from the Citrix Recording activity. You have to select the whole search area of the Google search bar. This time, it will ask you to indicate a point on the screen. Just point to the element that you have previously selected (in our case, it was the search bar area):

Click **OK**. Press **Save & Exit** and we are done. You can clearly see that UiPath generated the sequence shown in the following screenshot:

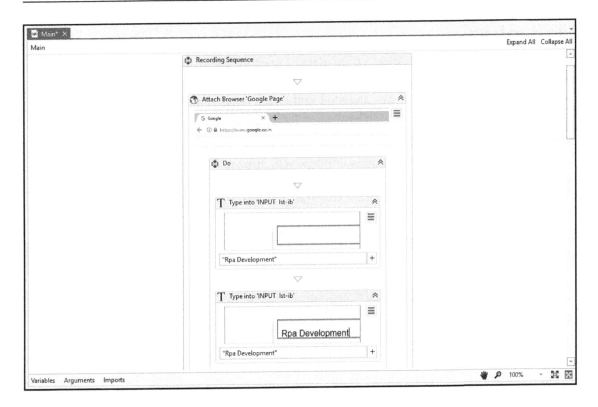

Press *F5* to see the result.

We have not used the **Open browser** activity. So, you have to log on to Google.com before executing this program. If you do not want this, then drag and drop the **Open Browser** activity before Recording Sequence.

Mail plugin

To use any Mail activities, you have to install the Mail package. To check whether the Mail package is installed or not, simply search for `Mail` in the **Activities** panel. It will list all the mail activities. If the activities are not listed in the **Activities** panel then you have to install the `UiPath.Mail.Activities` package.

To install the Mail NuGet package, click on the **Manage Package** icon at the top of the **Activity** panel. The **Manage Packages** window will appear. Search for `mail` in the search bar. As shown in the following screenshot, there is an **Uninstall** button next to **UiPath.Mail.Activities**. This is because the Mail activity is already installed in UiPath Studio. If it is not installed, an **Install** button will appear next to the **UiPath.Mail.Activities**:

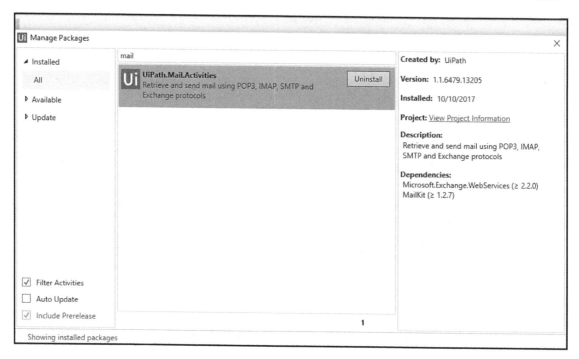

There are various mail activities that are used when working with UiPath Studio:

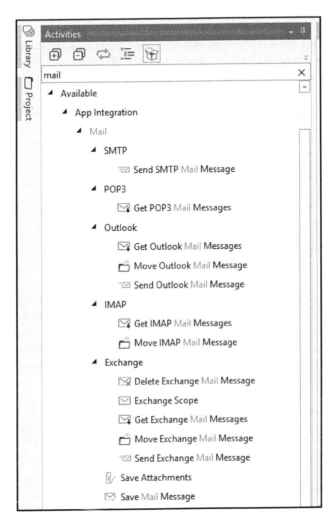

Some frequently used Mail activities are:

1. **SMTP**: It is used to send mail messages:
   - **Send SMTP Mail messages** activity: This activity is used to send a mail to another mail.

2. **POP3**: Although this is not the preferred choice, it is still used to receive mail messages:
   - **Get POP3 Mail Messages** activity: This activity is used to receive mail messages.

3. **IMAP**: It is used to receive mail messages. It is a better option than POP3:
   - **Get IMAP Mail Messages** activity: This activity is also used to receive the mail messages. It gives us the flexibility to manipulate mail messages and can be accessed remotely.

Once you get familiar with these, you can easily try the rest of the activities.

PDF plugin

PDF stands for **Portable Document Format** and it is used to keep the document platform independent. Why do we use PDF?

Suppose we have a Microsoft Word 2007 application installed in our system and we make a .doc file. This doc file can be opened on any system. Consider a system with Microsoft Word 2017 installed on it. If we view that doc file in this application, the format of the application is not going to be the same. This is because both Microsoft applications have different sets of architecture and specifications. Their format is not the same.

Here, PDF comes into action. It remains the same across all systems. That is why all confidential documents are sent or received using PDF. Also, if you do not want to change the behavior of the document across different platforms, you should convert the document into the PDF format.

To use any PDF activities, you have to install the PDF NuGet package. To check whether the PDF package is installed or not simply search for PDF activities in the **Activity** panel. It will list all PDF activities. If PDF activities are listed in the **Activities** panel, you have to install the UiPath.PDF.Activities package.

To install the PDF NuGet package, click on the **Manage Package** icon at the top of the **Activities** panel.

The **Manage Packages** window will appear. Search for PDF in the search bar. As shown in the following screenshot, there is an **Uninstall** button next to **UiPath.PDF.Activities**. This is because PDF activity is already installed in UiPath Studio. If it is not installed, an **Install** button will appear next to **UiPath.PDF.Activities**:

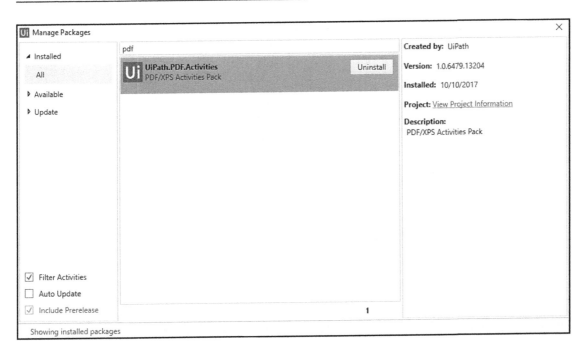

In our case, the PDF activity is already installed. That is why there is an **Uninstall** button.

Some frequently used PDF activities are:

1. **Read PDF Text**: It is used to read the text written on any PDF document. However, the **Read PDF Text** activity cannot guarantee extraction of the entire text.

OR

We can extract all the fields from the PDF file by using the Screen Scraping activity. Start scraping the PDF file by clicking on the Screen Scraping icon in the menu and simply locating the area in which we have to extract the data. If the text extraction fails, then change the extraction type to OCR with a scale of 3 and above. Choose either Google or Microsoft OCR.

2. **Read PDF with OCR**: It is used to read the image part of the PDF file. Suppose there is an image in the PDF file and there is some text written on it. The Read PDF text activity will fail to read that text. This is where OCR is used. There might be scenarios in which some text is written on a colorful background. Such cases can easily be tackled by using the **Read Text With OCR** activity.

If both **Read PDF Text** and **Read PDF with OCR** methods fail to extract the text, we still have the Screen Scraping method to extract the data from PDF (sometimes, we have to indicate the related element in order to recognize the text):

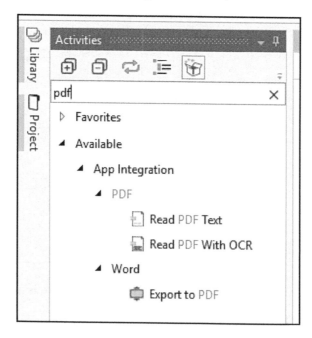

Select the proper method according to your needs and whatever is best suited to your project.

Web integration

Creating a web project, such as a company's website, B2B portal, or e-commerce website, requires the involvement of a wide range of technologies such as database design, networking, design, UX, user accessibility, SEO, and project management. These technologies also require HTML, CSS, JavaScript, JQuery, AJAX, system analysis and design, testing, operation, and a number of other methodologies. All of these activities can be classified under web integration.

Web integration, therefore, involves a wide process of connecting all these technologies and components that are essential for completing the web project.

The following are the methodologies that are used extensively for integrating with the web:

- **Application Programming Interface (API)**
- **Extensible Markup Language (XML)**
- **Simple Object Access Protocol (SOAP)**
- **JavaScript Object Notation (JSON)**
- **Representational State Transfer (REST)**

1. **API**: API integration is used quite frequently. It is impossible to find a modern web application or website that is not exposed to an API. API integration allows a software or web application to interact with other software or web applications in real time.

   UiPath Studio works both ways: It can automatically extract data from one application and pass it to a web service. Also, it can retrieve data from a web service and input it to another application.

   You have already explored and implemented how UiPath automates user interfaces. API is the easiest way to connect two applications or systems over the internet.

2. **XML**: XML is a markup language like **Hyper Text Markup Language (HTML)**. XML was designed to store and transport data and also to be self-descriptive. We can say that it extends the functionality of HTML. It is a software-independent and hardware-independent technique for storing and transporting data, for example:

   ```
   <Message><To>John</To>
      <From>Ava</From>
      <Subject>Reminder</Subject>
      < Message Body>Do not forget to meet me this
   weekend!</Message body></Message>
   ```

   You can make any Parent-Node structure in XML.

3. **SOAP**: SOAP is an XML-based messaging protocol for exchanging information between computers. You can say that SOAP is an application of XML.

The following are the advantages of SOAP:

- SOAP is a communication protocol designed to communicate over the internet.
- SOAP can extend HTTP requests.
- SOAP can be used for broadcasting a message.
- SOAP is platform-independent.
- SOAP is language-independent.
- SOAP is the XML way of defining what information is sent and how.
- SOAP enables client applications to easily connect to remote services and invoke remote methods. SOAP can also be used in a variety of messaging systems.

4. **JSON**: JSON is a method of lightweight data-interchange. It is self-describing and easy to understand. The most important part of JSON is that it is language independent.

When exchanging data between a browser and a server, the data can only be text. JSON is text-based. We can convert any JavaScript object into JSON, and send JSON to the server. Not only that; most languages have their methods for converting their objects into JSON and vice-versa.

We can also convert any JSON received from the server into JavaScript objects. In this way, we can work with the data as JavaScript objects, without any parsing.

5. **REST**: REST relies on a stateless, client-server, cacheable communication protocol. It is *an architectural style* for designing networked applications. The idea is that, rather than using complex techniques such as SOAP to connect between computers, a simple HTTP is used to make calls between machines.

The World Wide Web itself is based on HTTP and can be viewed as a REST-based architecture. RESTful applications use HTTP requests to post, read, and delete data. REST is lightweight. It is simple and fully-featured. That said, there is basically nothing you can do in web services that cannot be done with a REST architecture.

Excel and Word plugins

The most important plugins are Microsoft office plugins. In this section, we will cover Excel and Word plugins.

In most projects, one of these two plugins is used.

Excel plugin

Excel is an application program developed by Microsoft. It is a part of the Microsoft Office suite. Excel is capable of creating and manipulating files that are saved with .xls or .xlsx extensions. General uses of Excel include (an individual cell) cell-based calculation. For example, with an Excel spreadsheet, you can create a table, use formulae to compute every row and column, make your own monthly expense list, and so on.

Unlike a word processor such as Microsoft Word, Excel documents consist of rows and columns. Each column consists of a cell in which we can store a value. The value can either be text, string, or number.

In UiPath Studio, there is a NuGet Package called `UiPath.Excel.Activities`. The Excel activity is pre-installed in UiPath Studio. In case it is not installed, it can be installed manually.

To check if the Excel activity is installed or not, simply search for `Excel` activities on the **Activities** panel. It will list all Excel activities. If Excel activities are not listed in the **Activities** panel, then you need to install the **UiPath.Excel.Activities** package.

To install the Excel NuGet package, click on the **Manage Package** icon located at the top of the **Activities** panel.

A **Manage Packages** window will appear. Search for Excel in the search bar. As shown in the following screenshot, there is an **Uninstall** button next to **UiPath.Excel.Activities**. This is because Excel activities are already installed in UiPath Studio. If it is not installed, an **Install** button will appear next to **UiPath.Excel.Activities**:

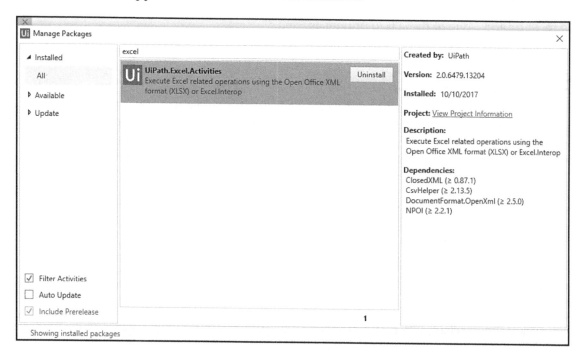

Word plugin

Microsoft Word is often called simply Word or MS Word. Microsoft Word is a widely used commercial word processor designed by Microsoft. Microsoft Word is a component of the Microsoft Office suite.

Microsoft Word is available for both Windows and Mac operating systems.

The following are the Microsoft Word features:

1. It makes it possible for everything displayed on the screen to appear in the same way when printed or moved to another program.
2. Microsoft Word has a built-in dictionary for spell checking.
3. Text-level features such as bold, underline, italic, and strike.

4. Page-level features such as paragraphing and justification.
5. Microsoft Word is compatible with many other programs, the most common being the other members of the Office suite.

In UiPath Studio, there is a NuGet package called **UiPath.Word.Activities**. Word activity is pre-installed in UiPath Studio. In case it is not installed, we have to install it manually.

To check whether the Word activity is installed or not, simply search for Word in the **Activities** panel and press **Enter**. It will list all the Word activities. If Word activities are not listed in the **Activities** panel then you have to install the **UiPath.Word.Activities** package.

To install the Word NuGet package, click on the **Manage Package** icon. The **Manage Packages** window will appear. Search for Word in the search bar. As shown in the following screenshot, there is an **Uninstall** button next to **UiPath.Word.Activities**. This is because Word activities are already installed in UiPath Studio. If it is not installed, there will be an **Install** button next to **UiPath.Word.Activities**:

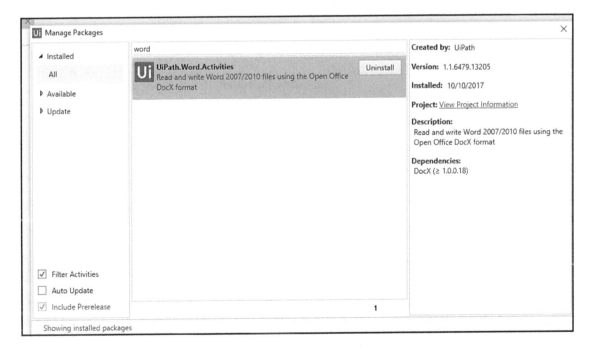

Credential management

In the Windows operating system, you can view your network login credentials, that is, the username and password, by using Credential Manager.

With the help of UiPath Studio, you can automate the process of creating, manipulating, and deleting credentials using some credential activities:

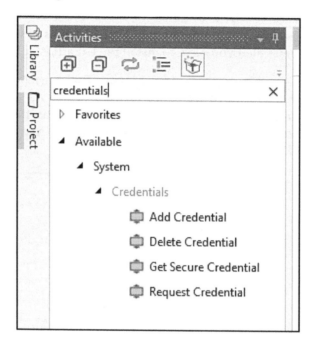

The following are credential activities:

1. **Add Credential activity**: You can add a credential activity for use in your project. You just simply have to specify the username and the password.
2. **Get Credential activity**: This activity is used to store the username and password for future use. It enables us to further check whether credentials are valid or not.
3. **Request Credential activity**: This activity is used to display a dialog box to a user asking them about their credentials. It then stores the username and password in string variables that can be further used to log in to the applications.
4. **Delete credential activity**: This activity is used to delete the credentials that we have stored.

Extensions – Java, Chrome, Firefox, and Silverlight

Extensions are small software programs that can be used to modify and extend the functionality of any browser. You can build your own extension by using web technologies such as HTML, JavaScript, and CSS. Extensions have little or no user interface.

Java extensions are useful when you have to automate a Java application. Without this extension, UiPath Studio does not correctly identify the UI element of a Java application.

Chrome and Firefox extensions are used when you are working with the Chrome/Firefox browsers. By this, we mean that while automating with UiPath Studio, if you are interacting with a browser, you first have to install the extension for that browser.

Similarly, the Silverlight extension has to be installed if you want to integrate your application using Microsoft's Silverlight.

Almost all extensions have a similar installation method. Once you get familiar with the method, you can install the remaining of the extensions on your own.

In UiPath Studio, you can find all the extensions in the **Setup Extensions** menu. Click on the **SETUP** tab at the top of the UiPath Studio window:

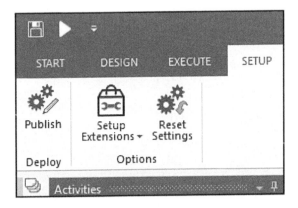

Now click on the **Set Up Extensions** icon and select the extension that you want to select:

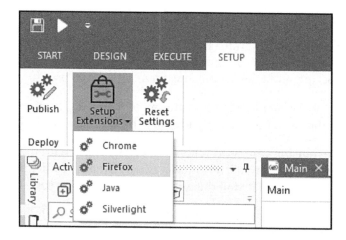

In this session, we are going to select the Firefox extension from the drop-down list. Automatically, the Firefox browser is opened and asks you to add UiPath. Just click on the **Add** button:

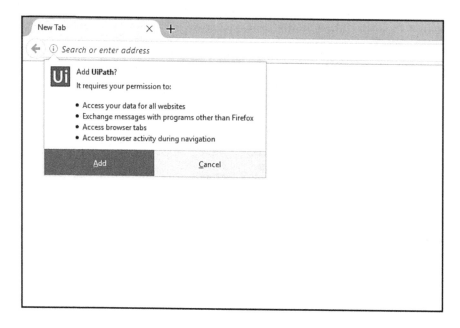

Your extension has been successfully installed. A dialog box will pop up confirming this.

If you want to install other extensions, you just have to select the desired extension from the drop-down list.

Summary

In this chapter, you have learned about the role of plugins and how they can increase the scope for automation. Over time, many new plugins will be introduced, the inclusion of those plugins and extensions will be on a similar line; however, the internal workings of those plugins may vary. You have also learned that the Terminal plugin is different from the PDF plugin. In this chapter, Java, Chrome, Firefox, and Silverlight extensions were also covered. You also learned about Mail, Web, and SAP integrations. Credential management was a nice addition to this chapter.

In the next chapter, we will focus on assistant bots and event triggers.

7
Handling User Events and Assistant Bots

In UiPath, there are two types of Robot that are used for automating any process. One is the back office Robot, which works in the background. It works independently, which means it does not require inputs from users or any user interaction. The other one is the **Front Office Robot**, which is also known as an **Assistant Robot**.

This chapter deals with front office bots. Here, we will learn the different ways in which events in the automation process can be triggered—by a simple press of a key, click of the mouse, and so on. To make things clearer, we will take examples of monitoring various events.

We will cover the following topics in this chapter:

- What are assistant bots?
- Monitoring system event triggers
- Monitoring image and element triggers
- Launching assistant bots on a keyboard event

What are assistant bots?

Assistant Robots are front office Robots that require some user interaction. In this case, the automation will run only when a certain event or user action is triggered.

Trigger events are basically commands to tell the Robot to start its automation process.

For example, say I want some text to be typed into the Notepad application. In particular, I want the Robot to type into the Notepad once I click on the text area (clicking being the trigger activity in this case) in the Notepad application.

Let us look at the following steps to understand more:

1. **Drag and drop the Monitor events activity**: Here, we drag and drop a **Monitor events** activity from the **Activities** panel inside which the trigger events will work; otherwise it will show you an error. The **Monitor events** activity looks like this:

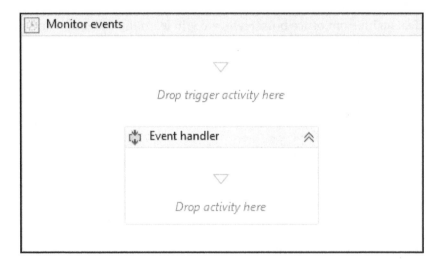

2. **Drag and drop the trigger activity of choice**: In the drop trigger area, drag and drop the trigger activity that you want.

There are a lot of trigger activities shown in the **Activities** panel. In this case, we will choose the **Click Trigger** activity:

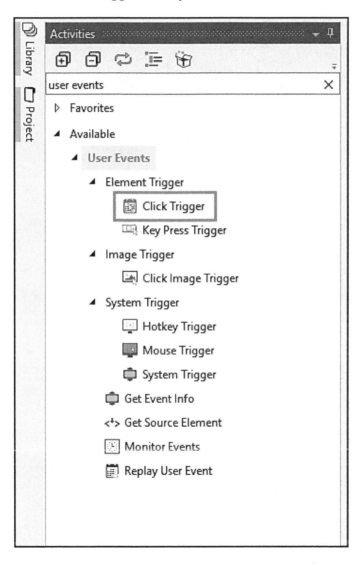

3. **Create workflow inside the Monitor events activity**: Now inside the **Event handler** space in the **Monitor events** activity, we have to create the workflow or the set of tasks we are required to do once the trigger activity works. In this case, we are using the **Type into** activity. Indicate the blank area of a Notepad window:

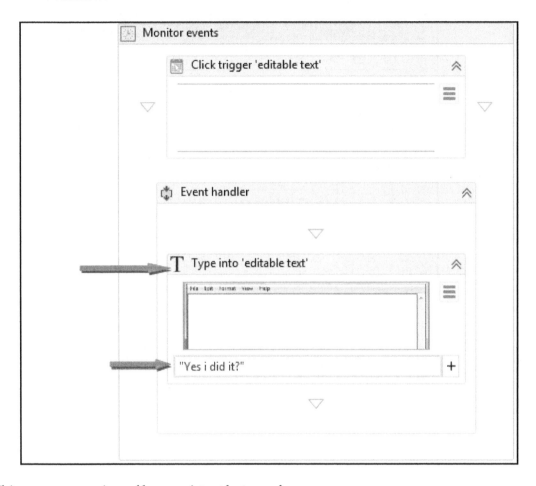

This was an overview of how assistant bots work.

Monitoring system event triggers

There are three system trigger events—**Hotkey Trigger**, **Mouse Trigger**, and **System Trigger**:

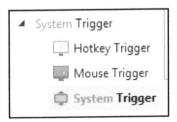

Though all three triggers are used for triggering activities, they are used differently as explained in the following section.

Hotkey trigger

Hotkey trigger works for shortcut keys. Suppose we want a certain workflow to work once the user presses the *Alt + F4* keys or any other shortcut key. In such a case, we will use the **Hotkey trigger**:

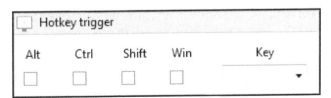

Mouse trigger

This is used when we want to trigger events on performing a mouse action (left-click, right-click, or middle-click) as shown in the following screenshot:

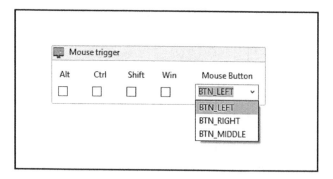

As shown in the screenshot, we can select the type of click with which we want to trigger events. We can also use other special keys with mouse actions as shown.

System trigger

This is the last type of system trigger activity. A system trigger is used to trigger events on mouse actions, keyboard actions, or both, all of which we can select from the **Properties** panel. We can also select the action to be performed, that is, forwarding the event or blocking the event as shown in the following screenshot:

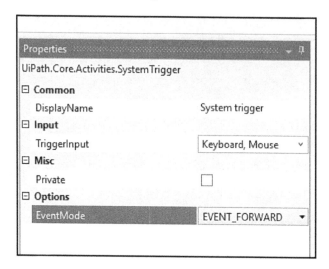

Monitoring image and element triggers

With an image trigger, the events will occur once the user has clicked on a certain image that is indicated in the **Click Image Trigger** activity.

By clicking on **Indicate element on screen**, we have to select an image that will trigger the event when clicked.

In the **Element Trigger**, there are two activities that come into play. These are **Click Trigger** and **Key Press Trigger** as shown in the following screenshot:

- The **Click trigger** activity is used to trigger events when a user simply clicks on a UI element:

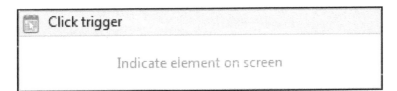

- The **Key press trigger** activity is used when we need to trigger events by pressing a certain key or by selecting the image on the screen to trigger events:

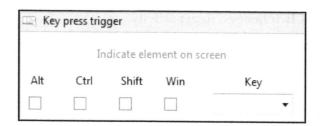

An example of monitoring email

To make things clearer, we will monitor a send email event through Gmail. The steps are listed as follows:

1. **Open the browser and browse to www.gmail.com**: To do this, drag and drop the **Open browser** activity. In the required field for the address, enter `www.gmail.com`:

2. **Getting username and password**: After typing in the address, we have to ask the user for a username and password. For this, we will use the **Input dialog** activity as shown in the following screenshot. We have dragged and dropped two **Input dialog** activities to ask the user for a username and password respectively. Until the user types in each dialog and presses okay, the Robot will not work:

Once the user types in the **username** and **password**, we save these details into two variables: user and pass. You can convert their values into a variable by going to the **Input dialog** property in the **Properties** panel. Just right-click on the empty text box of the **Result** property and choose **Create Variable**. We have named it **user** as shown in the following screenshot:

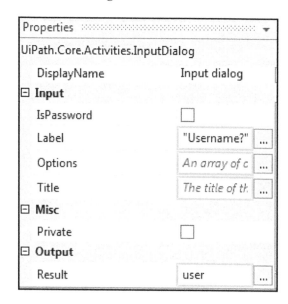

3. **Entering a username and password**: We shall use the **Type into** activity to enter a username and password by indicating the respective fields for typing in the username and password.

Once the user enters the username and password, he needs to login which he can either do by clicking on the login button or by pressing the *Enter* key on the keyboard. We will use the **Send hotkey** activity to send the *Enter* key (as shown in the following screenshot). By doing so, the login button is clicked:

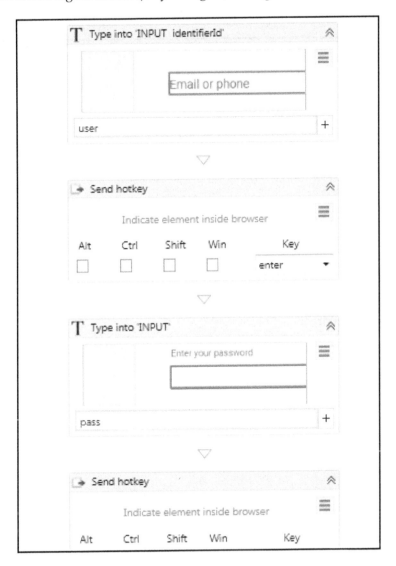

4. **Trigger the send email event with a Hotkey trigger**: Our next step is to trigger the send mail event. Here, pressing the *Enter* key will be the trigger. On pressing it, the Robot performs the rest of the send email task. For this, we will use the Hotkey trigger activity. We first have to drag and drop the **Monitor events** activity as trigger activities only work under it:

Since we are using the **Hotkey trigger**, we have dropped the **Hotkey trigger** activity in that area:

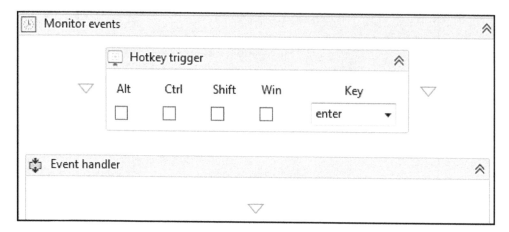

In the area for the **Event handler**, we need to give the sequence of steps for sending the mail, which will involve several steps. For this, we have created a workflow showing all the steps to be followed to send an email. This ranges from clicking on Compose mail to clicking on the Send button as explained in the following steps.

5. **Ask the user for the email ID of the recipient, the subject of the email, and its body**: Our next step is to ask the user for details. We will use three Input dialogs, one for the email ID, one for the subject, and one for the content.

As shown in the screenshot, we have used an Input dialog to obtain the recipient's email ID:

We now save the user input email ID inside a variable called name (you can easily create a variable by pressing *Ctrl + K* inside the **Output** box in **Properties**):

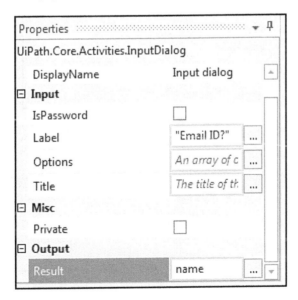

In the second **Input dialog,** we will ask the user to input the subject for the email:

The output, that is, the response entered by the user, is saved as a new variable called Subject? as shown in the following screenshot:

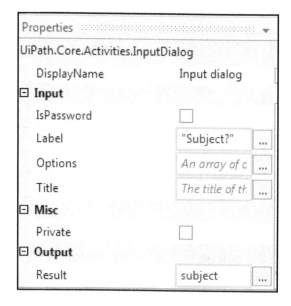

In the third input dialog, the user has to input the message/mail he or she wants to send:

We shall store the user output as a variable called `message`:

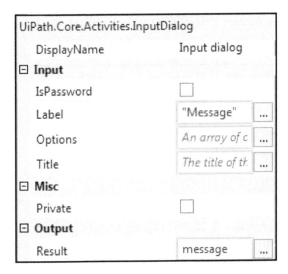

6. **Type in the details**: Now that we have all the details that are required for sending the mail, our next step will be to type into the required fields for sending the email. We will use the **Type Into** activity for this step:

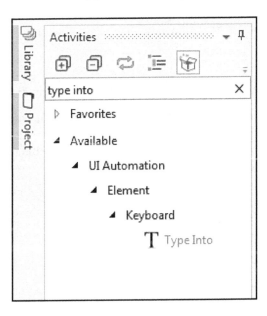

Drag and drop the **Type into** activity. Then, double-click on it and indicate the area where you want to type the email ID. Since we have saved the email ID as a variable, name, we enter this in the field provided, as shown in the following screenshot:

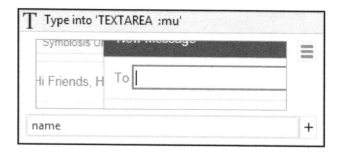

Our next requirement will be to indicate the area where we want to type the subject of the mail. Since we have saved the subject as a variable, Subject, we enter this in the field provided as shown in the following screenshot:

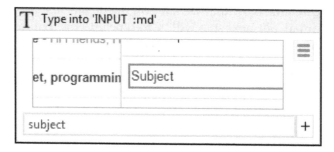

Now you are required to indicate the area where you want to type the message/mail as indicated in the screenshot. Since we have saved the content of the mail to be sent as a variable, message, we enter this in the field provided as shown in the following screenshot:

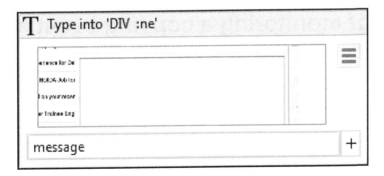

7. **Click on Send and confirm if successfully sent**: Our final step is to click on the **Send** button so that the mail is sent and the process is completed. In order to click on the **Send** button, we will use the **Click** activity and indicate the **Send** button. Doing so enables the Robot to easily recognize where to click:

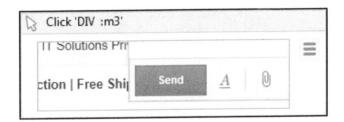

If you want, the Robot can also give a notification once the mail is sent. For this notification we will use the **Message box** activity, which will display the message, **message is sent**, as shown in the following screenshot. When the message is displayed, and after the user has pressed **OK**, the whole workflow will terminate since all of the steps have been executed:

Example of monitoring a copying event and blocking it

Let us take an example of monitoring a copying event and blocking it. In this example, we have an Excel file from which we want the data to be copied as soon as the user presses the *Enter* key:

1. **Drag and drop the Monitor events activity and the drop trigger activity into it**: Drag and drop the **Monitor events** activity. Double-click on it:

Drag and drop the **Hotkey trigger** activity and select the *Enter* key from the drop-down list, as shown in the screenshot:

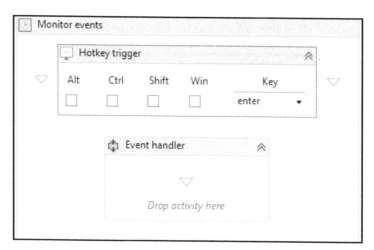

2. **Drag and drop an Excel application scope inside the Event handler portion**: We are required to drop an activity under **Event Handler**. In our case, the activity is copying data from Excel and pasting it. When we drag and drop the **Excel application scope** activity inside the **Event handler** and double-click on it, we see that first we have to browse to the Excel file from which we want to copy the information:

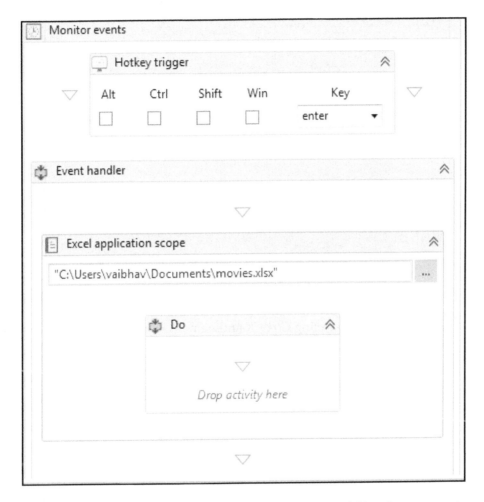

As shown in the screenshot, we have selected an Excel file whose name is movies; now we want to copy this file's content.

3. **Use the Read Range activity, extract the data and paste it into a new Excel file:**
   Now, inside the **Do** activity, drag and drop the **Read Range** activity to read all
   the data from this Excel file. We will keep this extracted data in a variable named
   movies, as shown in the screenshot:

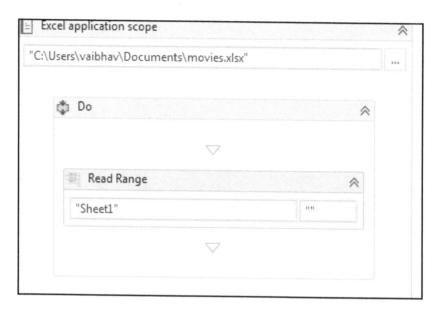

We have read the data from the Excel file. Next, we want to keep it in a variable.
For this, just click on the **Read Range** activity and go to the **Properties** panel. Then
create a variable by pressing *Ctrl + K* and name it movies:

4. **Append to another Excel file**: Now, since we have all the data saved, we can just drag and drop another Excel application scope. Then we will indicate the file that we want to append this data to. In the **Do** activity, just drag and drop the **Append Range** activity. Select the input as the variable we declared earlier, that is, movies as shown in the screenshot:

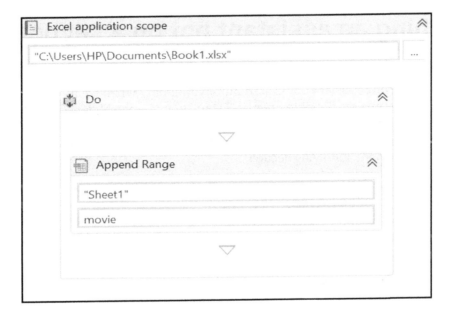

5. **Block the triggered event**: Now, in order to block triggered events you can select the EVENT_BLOCK event as the event type from the properties of the trigger in the **Properties** panel as shown in the following screenshot:

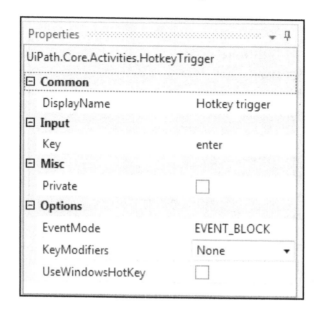

Launching an assistant bot on a keyboard event

Let us say we want our assistant bot to start automating only when we trigger an event. For example, the user wants his Robot to open and start typing in the Notepad window when he presses *Alt + W*. This can be achieved using the Hotkey trigger. Also, inside the Event handler, just create or record the sequence of steps to be followed. The detailed procedure has been explained in the following sections:

1. **Drag and drop the Monitor events activity**: In this step, we will just drag and drop the **Monitor events** activity into the workflow. When we double-click on it, it will look like this:

2. **Drag the Hotkey trigger activity**: In the next step, we will use the **Hotkey trigger** activity for the user to start the automation process. Assign *Alt + W* to the hotkey so that, when the user presses this hotkey, the event will be executed:

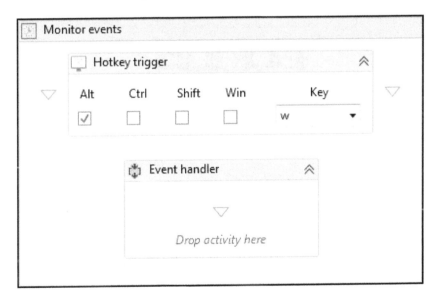

3. **Open Notepad and type into it**: Our final step is to record the sequence of the steps to be performed. In this case, this is to open Notepad and then type into it. For that just use the help of the **Desktop** recorder. First, we double-click on the Notepad application in the window as shown in the screenshot. Select the **ClickType** as **CLICK_DOUBLE** from the **Properties** panel:

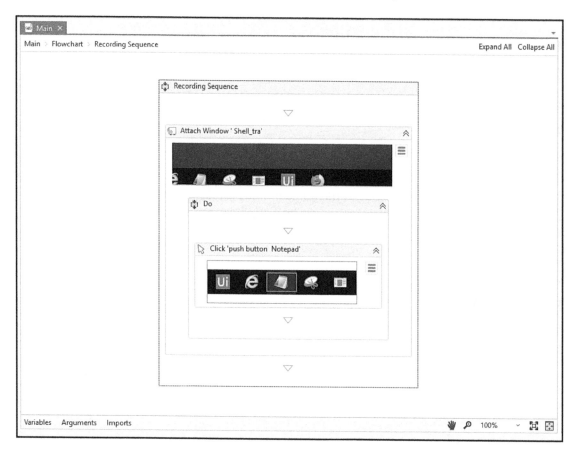

After that, we record the typing action and close the Notepad window. Then click on **Do not Save** because you do not want to save your file. The sequence is shown in the following screenshot:

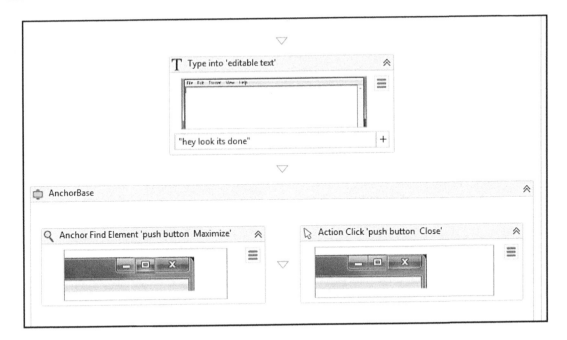

 We have also indicated the anchor to recognize the correct button to be clicked (in this case, the close window button's anchor is the maximize button). This makes it easier for the Robot to find the UI element.

Now, on pressing *Alt + W* the Robot will start executing the sequence.

Summary

In this chapter, we learnt about the assistant bot's utility. We also covered all the monitoring events that can be used to trigger actions and also saw examples of them. Once your automation program is made, there may still be problems that you are likely to face while executing it. To handle such scenarios, we will learn about Exception Handling in the following chapter.

8
Exception Handling, Debugging, and Logging

Sometimes, automation program may fail to execute. To deal with such cases, we use exception handling activities. In this chapter, we start with the various types of exception handling method available in UiPath, the exceptions that you may encounter, and how to deal with them. We will also learn about logging. An important topic covered in this chapter is debugging to check whether workflows are working properly or not and to rectify any errors.

Before we begin, let us look at the topics that will be covered in this chapter:

- Exception handling
- Common exceptions and ways to handle them
- Logging and taking screenshots
- Debugging techniques
- Collecting crash dumps
- Error reporting

Exception handling

Exception handling is a way to handle exceptions for a process that the program or the procedure has failed to execute.

For handling exceptions in a program, the best practice considered is to use the **Try catch** activity.

The **Try catch** activity can be found in the Activities panel. By dragging and dropping the **Try catch** activity into the workspace, we can handle exceptions. For handling errors in the **Try catch** block, we can divide the whole process into four parts just to make it simpler:

- Drag and drop the **Try catch** activity
- Try block
- Catch block
- Finally block

Let's build a Try catch block to handle exceptions, in following steps:

1. Drag and drop the **Try catch** activity: Create a blank project. Drag and drop the **Flowchart** activity into the Designer panel. Search for the **Try catch** activity in the **Activities** panel and drag it into the **Flowchart**. Set it as the **Start** node:

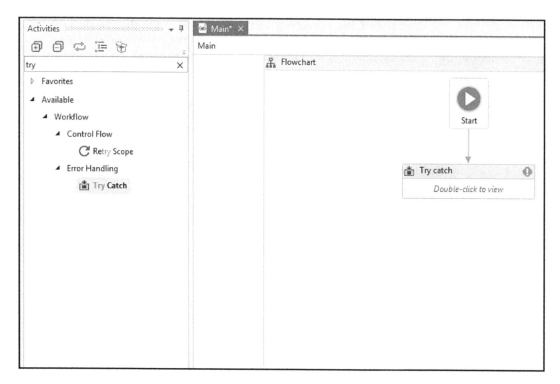

2. **Try**: When we double-click on the **Try catch** activity, dragged and dropped inside the workspace, space for the **Try** activity appears, as shown in the following screenshot:

Inside the **Try** block, we have to drop the activity we want to perform. Drop a **Write line** activity to test the working of **Try Catch** block, as shown in the following screenshot:

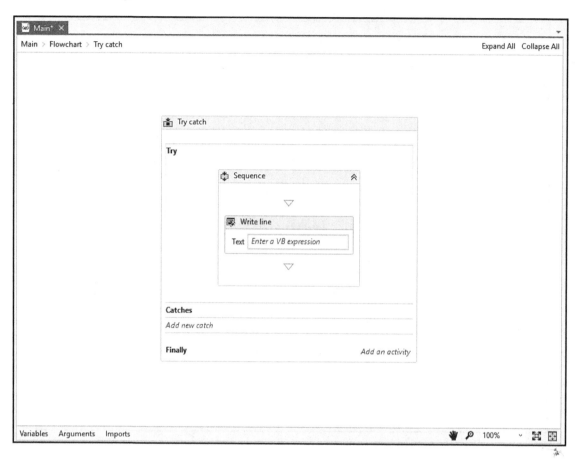

3. **Catches**: Inside the **Catches** activity, first we have to click on **Add new Catch** and then click on **Add Exception** option, from which we have to select the type of exception. In most cases, **System.Exception** is preferred. The following screenshot shows the types of exception. There are many more exceptions which can be viewed by clicking on the **Browse for Types** option:

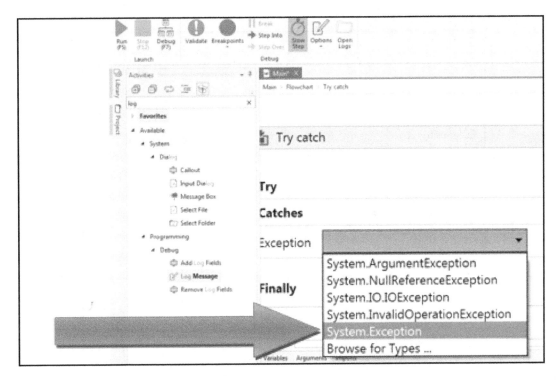

Exceptions that can be viewed when clicked on the **Browse for Types** option

Say the execution fails: for example, the **Click** activity is unable to be executed because of the unavailability of a UI element. In such a case, we can use the **Catches** block in order to either view the error that has occurred or for an alternative method to be used if that particular error occurs. As shown in the following screenshot, we will drop the activity in the **Catches** block. To print a message, we use a **Message box**:

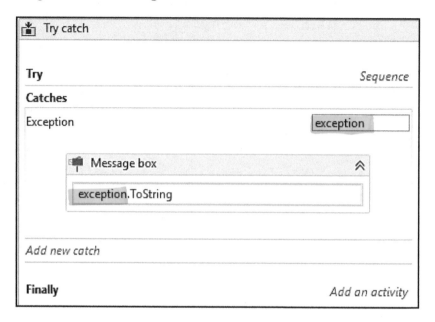

When we click on **Add new catch**, we are asked to select the type of exception. We have selected **System.Exception**. Now inside the exception block, we have dropped a **Message box** activity. Entering `exception.ToString` will display the error that occurred during execution.

4. **Finally**: When we have defined the exception for our sequence, the **Finally** block will always work, regardless of whether the execution was successful or not. Suppose we want to display a message to the user notifying that the process is complete. To make sure that the whole **Try catch** activity is executed, we will just drop a **Message box** activity in the area provided in the **Finally** block, as shown in the following screenshot:

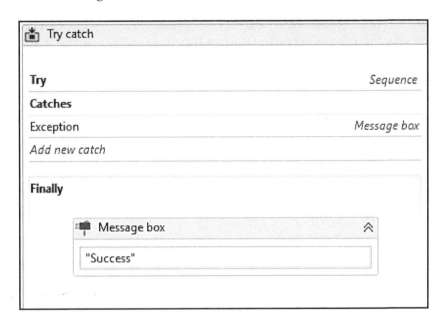

Common exceptions and ways to handle them

Implementing exception handling enables the robot to work in every possible situation and tackle any exception that may arise. There are some common exceptions that we usually face while working on UiPath.

Unavailability of UI element

When working on UiPath, especially on the web, we may encounter this type of error. This is because the UI element was not found due to the dynamic behavior of the web page. To handle this exception, we have to make changes in the selector attributes or we have to add new attributes to the selector so that the UI element can be easily found. For example, if we have a variable which is dynamically changing, we can use a wildcard so that it can be easily found by the robot. As shown in the following screenshot, we can edit the dynamic attribute of the selector using wildcard characters (in our case, *). Another way is to attach it to the live element:

Handling runtime exceptions

We may encounter runtime errors while working in UiPath. To rectify these errors, one of the best practices is to use the Try catch activity, which can be used to handle exceptions at runtime. By keeping an alternative inside the catch block, we can also overcome the error which we encountered before.

So placing your sequence or workflow inside the Try catch activity will help you handle runtime exceptions.

Orbit reference not set to the instant of an object

This type of error usually occurs when the default value required for some variable is not provided. In that case, we are required to give a default value to the required variable, as shown in the following screenshot.

In the empty area indicated in the following screenshot, just type the default value of the variable in order to overcome this error:

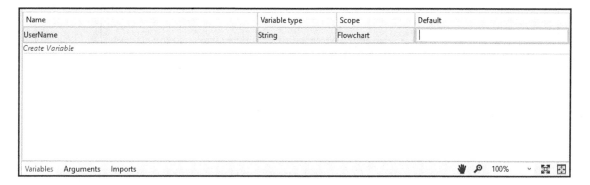

Index was outside the bounds of an array. Index out of the range

This error occurs when we try to iterate array elements by an index which is out of range. This happens when we are not aware of the size of the array and we just randomly type the index to access the element.

To resolve this, we must check the size of the indexes of the array or the collective list.

Image not found in the provided timeout

This type of exception is thrown because the image was not found. This may be due to a change of environment, such as resolution or theme settings. In this case, using some a selector attribute or indicating an anchor will work well:

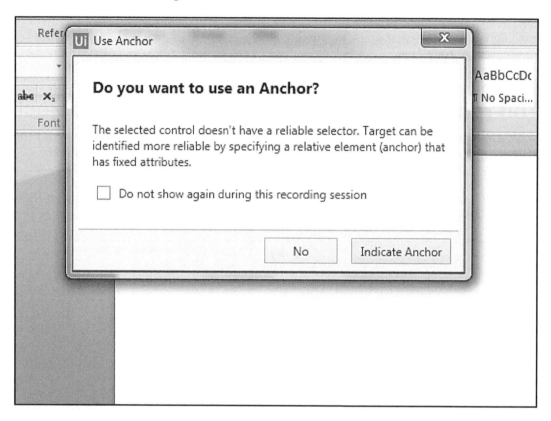

As shown in the preceding screenshot, when we cannot identify the image properly, **Indicate Anchor** will help us indicate the UI element nearby so that the recorder can identify the correct image.

Click Generic error - cannot use UI CONTROL API on this UI node please use UI Hardware ELEMENTS method

This type of error occurs when the environment in which we are trying to use the Click activity does not support Simulate or Send message activity (used by us to click the UI element).

Sometimes, either **SimulateClick** or the **SendWindowMessages** may be checked. In both cases, when an exception is thrown we just have to uncheck the appropriate box.

Logging and taking screenshots

UiPath has a multi-process architecture that offers to execute each workflow separately in the executor. Executors are managed by UI robots. So, if any executor stops working, then the entire process will not be affected.

Client logging

Client logs basically enable a server to record connections. These logs can be used by content providers in various scenarios, such as to generate billing, to trace media server usage, or to deliver suitable quality content depending on the speed of the client's server.

For client logging in UiPath, we have an NLog configuration file which makes it easy and flexible to integrate with databases, servers, or any other NLog targets. Logging can be configured with this `NLog.config` file. UiPath Studio, Robot, and workflow execution generate log messages on the client side:

- Messages which are produced by the workflow execution are logged with the execution logging source. Messages produced by UiPath Studio are logged as Studio Source and those produced by UiPath Robot are logged as Robot logging Source.
- We can also access these logs from UiPath Studio.

We can access the stored logs by clicking on **Open Logs** in the **EXECUTE** option.

By default, these Logs are saved in `%Local App %\Uipath\Logs`:

- The automatic logging mechanism for all errors generated, including values of variables and arguments, may be enabled in the `UiRobot.exe` config file, which is present in `C:\Users\USername\AppData\Local\UiPath\app-17.1.6435`, by setting the Log parameter from `0` to `1` inside the `<Switches>` section.
- We have two activities that can be used for logging and these are the Log message and **WriteLine** activities.

Server logging

If you have configured the UiPath server, then all logs generated by the execution are also sent to the server.

You can take a screenshot anytime by pressing *Ctrl + PrtScrn*.

Debugging techniques

There are various techniques provided by UiPath Studio for debugging in order to check whether the workflow is running successfully or to find out errors in order to rectify them. At the top of the UiPath window, we can see various available methods of debugging inside the **EXECUTE** block, as shown in the following screenshot:

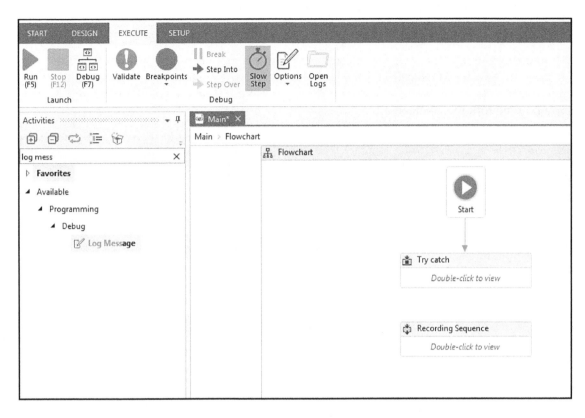

As shown in the preceding screenshot, there are various techniques for debugging. They are:

- Setting breakpoints
- Slow step
- Highlighting
- Break

Setting breakpoints

While debugging a workflow, we can set breakpoints in between if we want to run the program up to a specific location. This is useful when we have to stop before an activity ends completely. In such a case, we should use a breakpoint on the previous activity, as shown in the following screenshot:

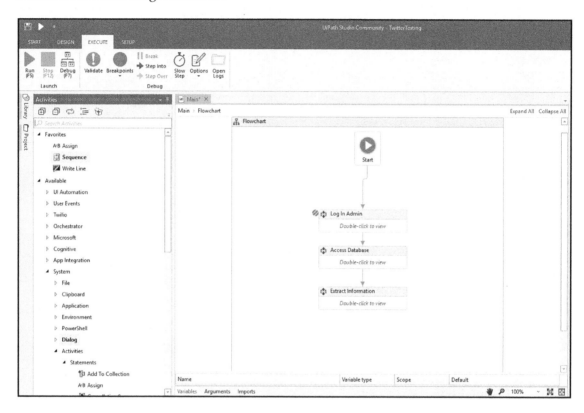

The highlighted region indicates the breakpoint since the execution stops just after the breakpoint. In order to continue any further, we have to click on the **Continue** button on the top corner indicated by the arrow:

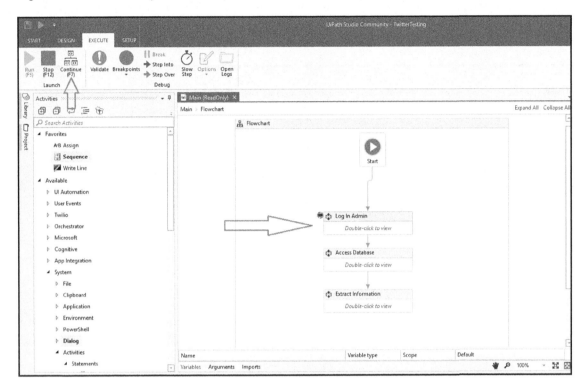

When we click on **Step into**, the relevant part will start to execute; after we click on **Step over**, execution will jump to the next part, and so on.

Slow step

This is an activity in the **EXECUTE** block through which we can reduce the execution speed of a particular process or activity. This way, we can identify each and every process and keep an eye on where to find the error. In the Output panel, all activities or steps can be viewed. The following screenshot shows how to use the **Slow step** activity:

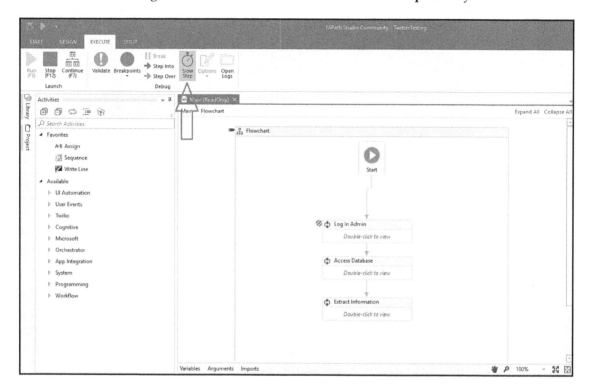

As indicated by the arrow in the preceding screenshot, when we click on **Slow step** the execution time for this particular step increases.

Highlighting

Highlighting is used to highlight the steps we have taken during automation and to identify each and every step in the workflow. It is very useful while debugging and its panel can be found in the **Options** menu of the **Execute** section in the Ribbon:

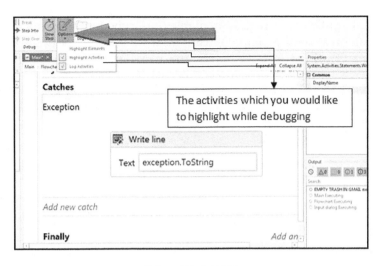

Various activities for highlight.

Break

The Break activity is used to break a process at a certain point. Suppose we have a sequence performing seven activities together and we want to break the execution at a certain activity. For this, we can use the **Break** activity, as shown in the following screenshot:

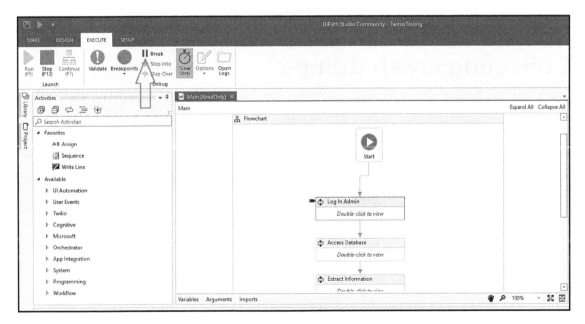

While debugging, an option for **Break** is available (indicated by the arrow in the preceding screenshot). We can break at any point we want to. If we want to continue any further, we just have to click on **Continue**, as indicated by the arrow in the following screenshot:

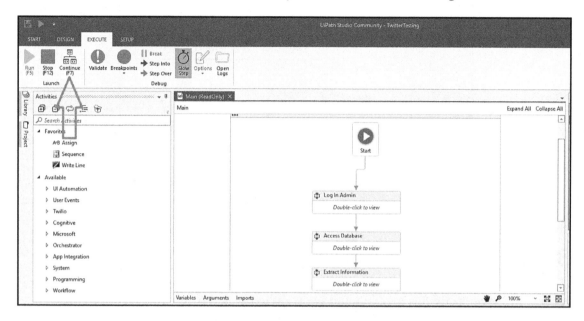

Or we can stop the execution at that point by clicking on the **Stop** option.

Collecting crash dumps

Collecting crash dumps basically refers to collecting information when your UiPath Studio crashes. We can enable and disable crash dumps. These dumps provide us with information regarding the UiPath crash.

Memory dumps are of two types—**full dumps** and **minidumps**. Full dumps provide us with complete information about the encountered crash while minidumps provide us with just the main information regarding the crash.

When a crash is encountered, we first have to identify the process which has crashed. Usually, a dialog will appear on the screen indicating the nature of the crash and the application involved. A UiPath process could crash, such as UiStudio.exe, Uiexplorer.exe, or Uilauncher.exe, or the target application you want to automate may crash.

Enabling crash dumps

The following are the steps to enable crash dumps:

1. To enable crash dumps, we first have to download the `EnableFullDump.erg` file for full dumps from `https://cdn2.hubspot.net/hubfs/416323/QuickAnswers/EnableFullDump.reg?t=1513326308120` or the `EnableMiniDump.erg` file from `https://cdn2.hubspot.net/hubfs/416323/QuickAnswers/EnableMinDump.reg?t=1513326308120`

2. Double-click the file and click Yes. Administrator rights are needed to access the registry settings

3. The dumps folder is `%TEMP%` whose complete path is like `C:\\users 2;username\AppData\Local\TEMP`

4. When the application crashes, you will find the `.dmp` file in the `TEMP` folder. For example, if UiExplorer crashes then a file such as `UiExplorer.exe.7429.dmp` will be found in the `TEMP` folder

Disabling crash dumps

To disable crash dumps, perform the following steps:

1. Download the `DisableDump.reg` file from `https://cdn2.hubspot.net/hubfs/416323/QuickAnswers/DisableDump.reg?t=1513326308120`.

2. Double-click the file and click Yes to disable crash dumps, Administration rights are needed for this action.

Error reporting

A user may encounter an error in UiPath and want to report it. As mentioned before, there are two types of customer for UiPath:

- Enterprise Edition customers
- Community Edition customers

Enterprise Edition customers

If you are an Enterprise customer, then you can report the error to the UiPath community in a very simple way:

1. Just go to this link: `https://www.UiPath.com/contact-technical-and-activations`.
2. You will be re-directed to a page where you have to fill out a simple form containing some basic details and then upload the file in which the error is encountered, as shown in the following screenshot.
3. After uploading, just click on the **Submit** button. UiPath will respond to you with the proper solution:

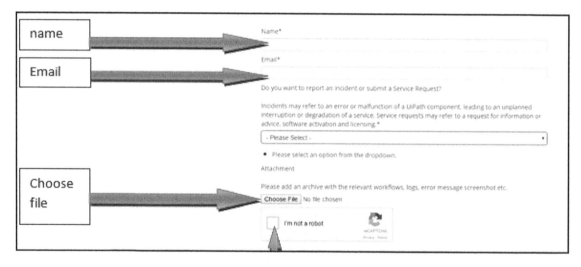

Details that need to be filled while uploading the encountered error file

Community Edition users

Since the Community Edition is free, UiPath does not provide support to Community Edition users. However, all solutions to errors encountered can be found by going to the UiPath forum. All types of errors and their solutions are properly discussed in the forum. You can also go to the resources page and find the solution to your problem.

For this, visit `https://forum.UiPath.com/`:

Resource page

Summary

In this chapter, you have learned how to use exception handling techniques and log error screenshots, and other useful information to be used for debugging or reporting. You have also learned how to debug code.

You have learned how to make an automation project, as well as how to use exception handling. Your learning, however, does not end here. In the next chapter, we will refine your learning by teaching you best practices for managing and maintaining your code.

Managing and Maintaining the Code

9

Just creating an automation project is not enough. It is important to have your project organized in a proper way—whether it is deciding which layout to use, or naming your steps properly. A project can also be reused in a new one, making it very convenient for the user. This chapter explains ways in which we can reuse projects. We will also learn about configuration techniques and see an example. Finally, we will learn how to integrate the TFS server.

Listed are the topics that will be covered in this chapter:

- Project organization
- Nesting workflows
- Reusability of workflows
- Commenting techniques
- Sate Machine
- When to use Flowchart, State Machine, or Sequence
- Using config files and examples of config files
- Integrating the TFS server

Project organization

While working on any automation project, it is very important to work with a proper set of rules so that the project can be organized in an efficient way. In UiPath, the following are some of the best practices considered while working on a project:

- Pick an appropriate layout for each workflow
- Break the whole process into smaller parts
- Use exception handling
- Make your workflow readable
- Keep it clean

We will now elaborate on each of the best practices.

Picking an appropriate layout for each workflow

There are various layouts available while creating a new project. Among those layouts, we have to choose the best option on the basis of the type of automation process we are undertaking. All the layouts are shown in the following screenshot:

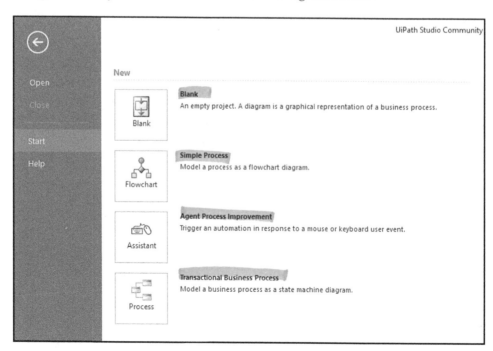

Blank

A Blank project is simply a blank page on which you can create the type of layout you want. That is, you can simply start with a Sequence activity if your workflow is in a single order/sequence or you can use a Flowchart activity if you have a bigger or more complex workflow to be designed. It depends on the needs of the user or the type of automation to be undertaken. The following screenshot shows a Blank project:

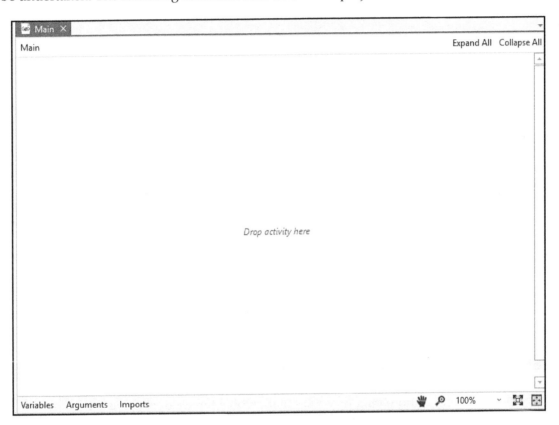

Simple process

The simple process is a layout that is used to model a process as a flowchart diagram in which there is space for user input. Inside this, we can use a sequence that processes the required input in a further transaction process. If there is no new input for the transaction, it will end the process; inside the transaction process, we have to make a workflow that can be used to automate it. This is by default a generated process that can be deleted or changed if required. An example of a simple process has been shown in the following screenshot:

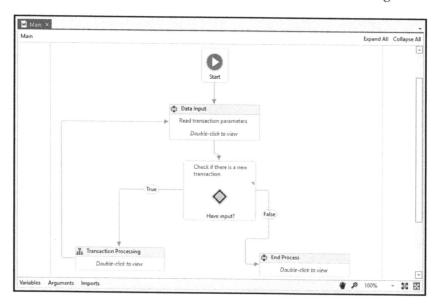

Agent process improvement

This triggers the automation in response to a mouse or keyboard user event. It is basically used when the user is automating processes that involve typing or clicking actions. A simple layout that appears in this process is shown in the following screenshot:

Transactional business process

We will use this layout if we want to model a business process as a State Machine diagram. It is basically a demo of how transactional business process automation works. If we want to build a better Robot to automate such processes, it is better to use this layout.

This layout is categorized into different states:

- **Init**: In **Init** state, we have to configure our settings, credentials (if any), and initialize all the variables that are going to be used in this transaction. All configuration files of the applications (being used in this transaction), are read and taken into account by the robot. The **Init** state also invokes all the applications that are used in the transaction.

- **Get Transaction Data**: In this state, all the transaction data is fetched from the **Init** state. If there is no transaction data, then it transfers the control to **End Process** state.
- **Process Transaction**: In this State, all the transaction data is processed.
- **End Process**: This state ensures that all the processes are completed and there is no transaction data available. It also closes all the applications that are used in the transaction:

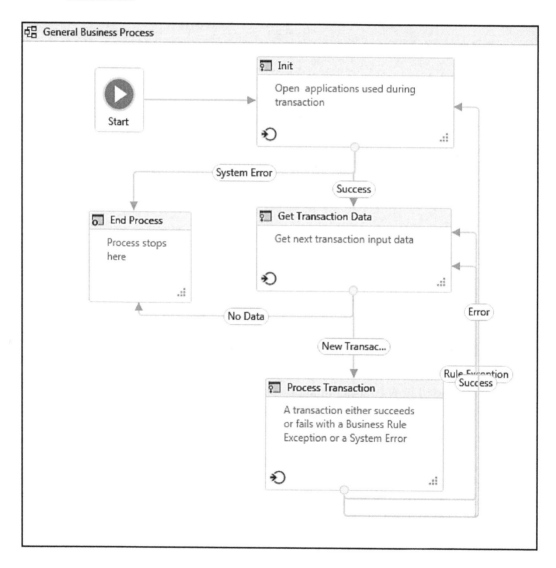

Breaking the process into smaller parts

To build any project, we have to use various activities. But using too many activities makes the project clumsy and it is not readable. We have to design our project in such a way that each independent part resides alone. We can achieve this by using workflows.

We should put each independent part of the project inside a single workflow. We can invoke all the workflows inside the project at the appropriate position.

Dividing the project into workflows makes the project cleaner and more maintainable. Now, if any developer wants to debug your code, they can check the different workflows and easily pinpoint in which workflow a particular error occurred. If the project is not divided into workflows, it will be a nightmare for the developer to fix any error.

Thus, breaking an automation into smaller parts enables easy debugging, as well as the workflows across projects:

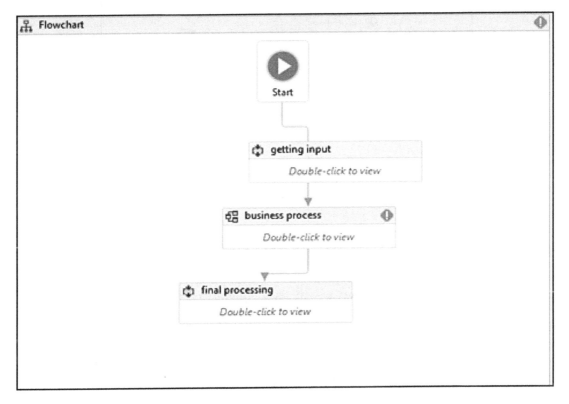

Flowchart of breakdown of automation and reusing workflows across projects

Using exception handling

While working on a project, it is better to use exception handling because it reduces the risk of errors. For instance, using the **Try catch** block can give you a proper error message, which helps us handle exceptions. There are various exception handling techniques that have been explained earlier and that are very useful while working on a project. An example featuring using the **Try catch** activity to handle exceptions has been shown in the figure. Here, we have used the **Write line** activity to display messages in the case of any error detected by the **Catch** block or the **Finally** block (as highlighted in the screenshot):

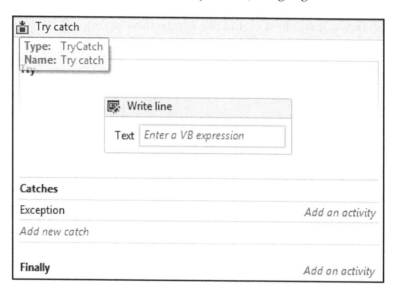

Making your workflow readable

It is good practice to name activities on the basis of the operations they perform to ensure that when we return to the workflow, we can easily identify each and every step used in it. This becomes very helpful while finding and resolving errors as it specifies the process when showing an error during debugging. If activities are properly named, we get to know exactly which part of the workflow is not working. For example, we will create a workflow that will ask the user to guess a number, on the basis of which we will perform an addition and finally display the answer. The following screenshot shows the proper naming of the steps involved in the process:

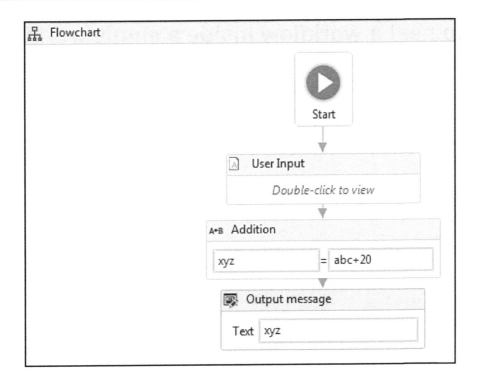

Keeping it clean

Just as writing in a clean and understandable manner is the quality of a good coder, the same holds true for an RPA developer. Clean code helps us understand the whole process very easily—you and whoever is reading it.

Nesting workflows

While working in UiPath, it is better to divide the whole process into smaller parts and then nest these workflows into a larger one or the **Main** workflow. This can be done using the **Invoke workflow file** activity given in the **Activities** panel. There are several steps involved in nesting a workflow or many workflows into a single workflow.

How to nest a workflow inside a single workflow

Say we have two workflows. In this example, we will invoke one workflow into the other:

1. Add an **Invoke workflow file** activity to the first workflow:

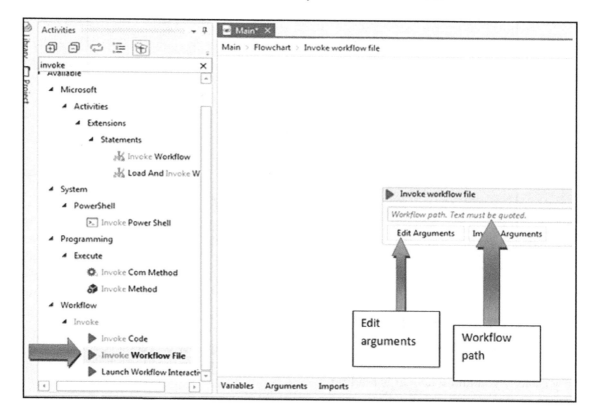

Screenshot of Invoke workflow file

2. Click on the **Edit Arguments** option available.
3. Define an argument and type it in the Invoke workflow arguments that appear:

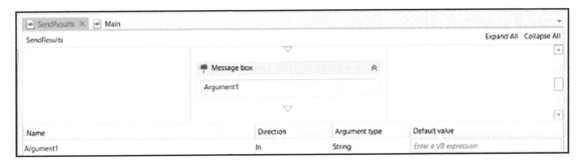

Invoke workflow arguments

4. In the **Arguments** panel in the second workflow, create an argument with the same name as the first workflow. You will now be able to use that argument as any other variable.

Reusability of workflows

Reusing workflows makes the automation process easier and better since we can use earlier created workflows in our project that we are trying to use for automation. There are two methods for this:

- Invoke workflow file
- Templates

Invoke workflow file is a good process if we have a complex automation project. We can divide it into smaller parts. By using the **Invoke workflow file** activity, we can invoke all those files in our project and collect all these smaller parts in a single workflow. However, if we want to invoke a previously created workflow in our project and make changes to the latter, the former will also get affected. Hence, it is recommended to use the **Invoke workflow file** activity only when we have a complex workflow:

image to be added here

As shown in the preceding screenshot, the **Invoke workflow file** activity requires the path to its associated XAML file.

Invoke workflow file

Invoke workflow file is a good process if we have a complex automation project. We can divide it into smaller parts and then, by using the **Invoke workflow file** activity, we can collect all these smaller parts in a single workflow file. However, if we want to invoke previously created workflows in our new workflow and make changes to the new workflow, the previous workflow will also get affected. Hence, it is recommended to use the **Invoke workflow file** activity only when we have a complex workflow and we want to divide the process into smaller parts and then use them together. There is another property for that, what we need here; it's as follows:

As shown in the preceding screenshot, the **Invoke workflow** activity requires a variable expression. We can create a variable and set a timeout that is required for the **Invoke workflow file** activity.

Templates

Saving the workflow as a template helps you preserve the original workflow file. So whatever modifications you made in the template, no changes will be made in the original workflow. We often use templates when creating small pieces of common automation that are reusable and applicable in multiple workflows. So you can use templates if the workflow does not change over time. The most common example is when you create your own reusable snippets using data, data tables, and .xml files.

Adding a workflow as a template

Follow the steps given to add a workflow as a template, which is explained as follows:

1. Add a new folder in the **Library**:

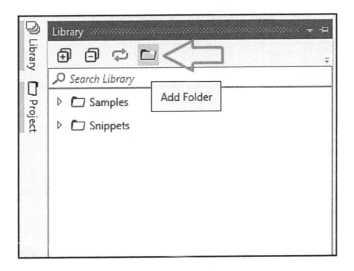

2. After clicking on the **Add Folder** icon you can browse for your file containing the workflows. Just select folder from the list that contains all the workflows. Now the folder can be used anytime in any workflow from the **Library** panel.

3. We can also remove an added file by just right-clicking on it and then selecting the **Remove** option, as shown in the following screenshot:

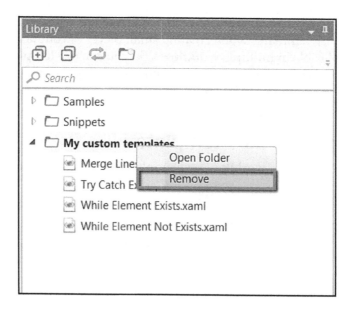

Commenting techniques

Using comments in workflows is considered a good practice as it can give a better step-by-step notification of what is done in the workflow. Therefore, commenting in a complex workflow is considered to be good while debugging:

- The package you'll need to use comments inside a workflow needs to be installed from the Package Manager functionality that is available in the **Activities** panel (the **Manage Packages** icon). You can install **UiPath.Core.Activities** from the packages; inside you will find the **Comment** activity in the **Activities** panel as indicated by the arrow (in this case, it is installed):

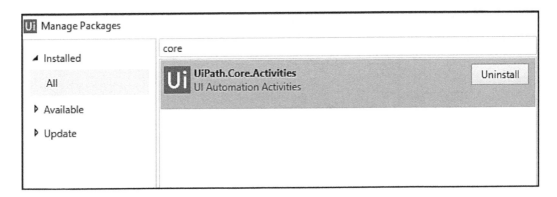

- Once the package is installed, just drag and drop the **Comment** activity from the **Activities** panel and add comments in between the workflows wherever you want:

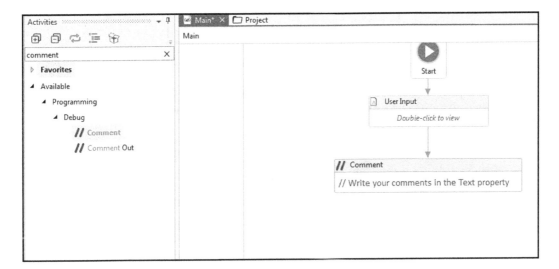

State Machine

A State Machine uses a finite number of sets in its execution. It can go into a state when it is triggered by an activity; it exits that state when another activity is triggered. Another important aspect of State Machines is transactions. They enable you to add conditions based on which transactions jump from one state to another. These are represented by arrows or branches between states.

There are two activities specific to State Machines. They are **State** and **Final State**, and they are shown in the following screenshot:

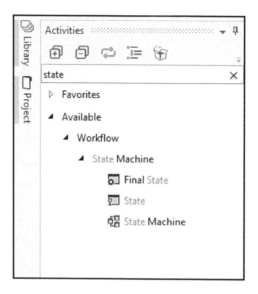

The **State** activity consists of three sections—**Entry, Exit,** and **Transitions**, while the **FinalState** only contains **Entry**. We can expand these activities by double-clicking them to view more information and to edit them:

- **FinalState** activity: This activity contains all those activities that need to be processed when the state is entered:

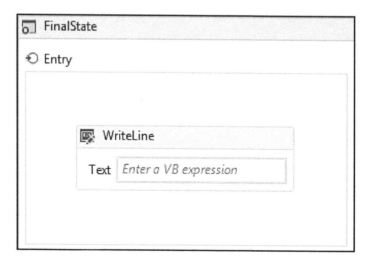

- **State** activity: Transitions contain three sections—**Trigger**, **Condition**, and **Action**, which enable you to add a trigger for the next state or a condition under which an activity is to be executed:

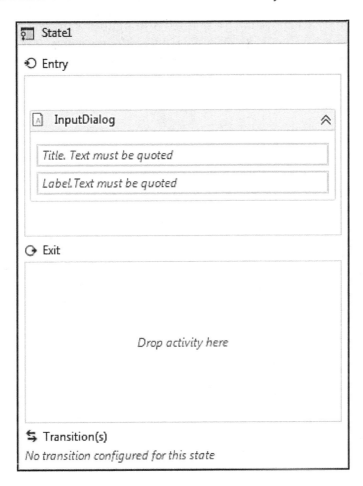

When to use Flowcharts, State Machines, or Sequences

A Sequence is used only when we have a selected a straightforward set of instructions on how to create a workflow. That is, we do not have to make decisions. It is preferred when we are recording some steps in a sequential manner and we are creating a simple workflow. One such sequence is shown in the following screenshot:

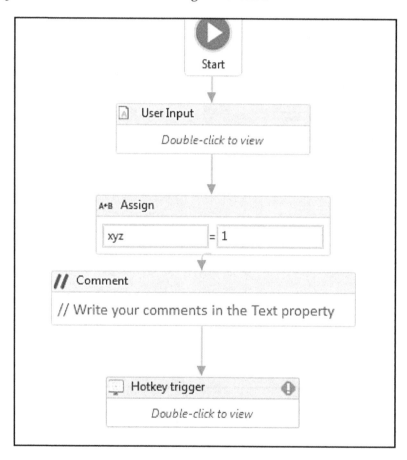

Now, when it comes to State Machines and Flowcharts, both are used for complex processes and both work well. They work in the same manner, but State Machines have some advantages over Flowcharts, which are listed as follows:

- Complex transitions are much clearer with State Machines as they have an inbuilt layout of the workflow.
- Flowcharts do not inherently have the concept of waiting for something to happen. State Machines do (a transition will not occur until a trigger completes and the condition evaluates to true).
- State Machines naturally encapsulate the action group:

Using config files and examples of a config file

When it comes to configuration, UiPath does not have any pre-built configuration file such as Visual Studio, but we can create one. It is considered to be one of the best practices to keep environment settings in a config file so that they can be easily changed by the user when required. Thus, when we create a project, the project.json file that holds all the activities is created automatically. Project.json can be found in the folder where the project is saved. To access the folder, we can just open the **Project**, then copy the path (as shown in the following screenshot), and paste it into File Explorer:

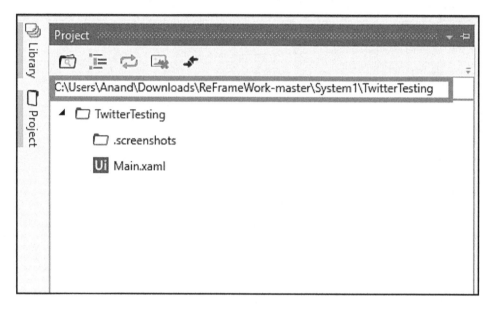

Then you can see a `project.json` file in File Explorer like the one shown in the following screenshot:

Name	Date modified	Type	Size
Initialization	11/14/2017 1:28 PM	XAML File	5 KB
Main	11/14/2017 1:28 PM	XAML File	36 KB
project	11/14/2017 1:28 PM	JSON File	1 KB
Transaction	11/14/2017 1:28 PM	XAML File	9 KB

The following screenshot displays the code inside the `project.json` file, when you open that file in Notepad:

```json
{
    "name": "a",
    "description": "Transactional Business Process Project",
    "main": "Main.xaml",
    "dependencies": {},
    "excludedData": [
        "Private:*",
        "*password*"
    ],
    "toolVersion": "17.1.6522.14204",
    "projectVersion": "1.0.6527.24239",
    "packOptions": {},
    "runtimeOptions": {}
}
```

You can also store your settings with the help of a spreadsheet or credentials. There are various parameters contained in the `project.json` file. They are:

- **Name:** This is the title of the project that is provided when creating a project in the create New Project window:

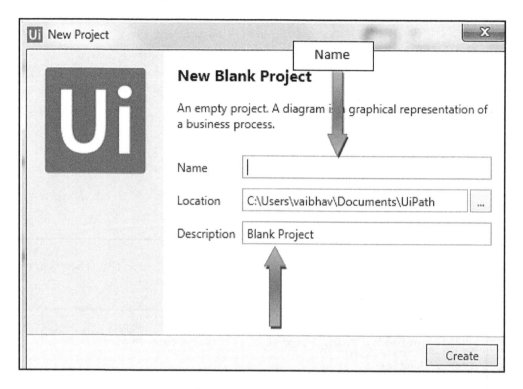

- **Description**: When creating a project, a description is also required. You can add the description in the Create New Project window, as shown in the preceding screenshot.

- **Main**: This is the entry point for the project. It is saved as `main.xml` by default, but you can change its name from the **Project** panel. Also, you have multiple workflows for a project, it is necessary to attach all these files to the main file with the **Invoke Workflow File** activity. Otherwise, those files will not be executed:

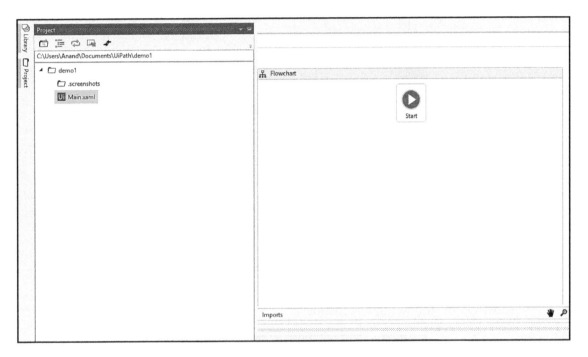

- **Dependencies**: These are the activities packages that are used in a project and their versions.
- **Excluded data**: Contains keyword that can be added to the name of an activity to prevent the variable and argument values from being logged at the verbose level.
- **Tool version**: The version of Studio used to create a project.

- **Adding Credential**: We can add particular settings that can be used further. For example, we can save the username and password to be used further, so this can be done with the help of the **Add credential** activity that can be found in the **Activities** panel, as shown in the following screenshot:

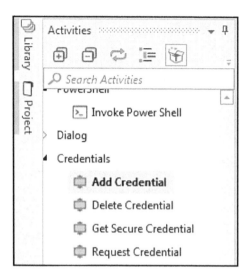

After adding credentials, type the required values in the **Properties** panel, as shown in the following screenshot:

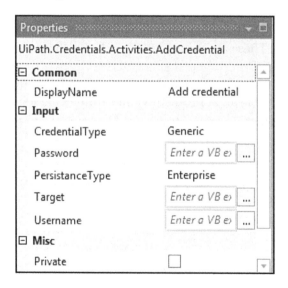

So, when the credentials are set, we can delete, secure, or request credentials, as shown in the following steps:

1. **Delete Credentials**: If we want to delete a credential then we can just drag and drop the **Delete Credentials** activity and then define the target for the credential:

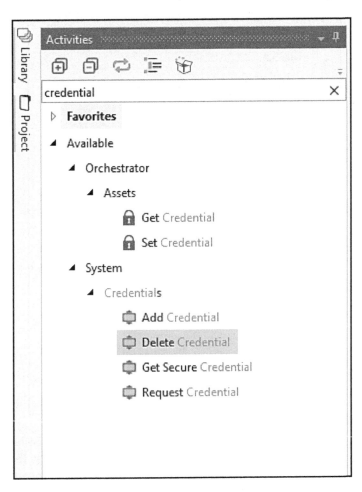

2. **Get Secure Credential**: This is used to get the values, that is, the username and password, that were set during the addition of a credential. We have to set the target the same as before; the output will be the username and password:

3. **Request Credential**: This is a property in which the robot displays a message dialog asking the user for username and password and stores this information as a string. This can then be used in further processes. The user can select OK to provide credentials or even cancel it if they do not want to provide credentials.

Integrating a TFS server

UiPath integrates a series of actions that allow us to have better collaboration on the project. Inside the **Project** panel, by right-clicking on the file we can see a list of properties that are included in it:

- By clicking on the **Get Latest Version** option, we can get the latest version of the selected file from the TFS server
- You can also rename or delete an existing file
- To edit a Read Only workflow, you can select; **Check Out** for edit
- To check in changes, select **Check In** from the menu

Summary

This chapter covered the organization of projects, modularity techniques, workflow nesting, and using the TFS server to maintain a version of source code. In the final chapter, you will gain insight into how you deploy and manage your bots using the Orchestrator.

10
Deploying and Maintaining the Bot

On completion of an automation project design, we make use of the Orchestrator to manage our bots. Before that, we publish our workflow first using the publish utility. Once we publish the project, the package is uploaded to the server. Then we use Orchestrator to manage any number of bots for any number of tasks. The Orchestrator Server also provides the facility for scheduling bots and specifying the time intervals that they work in according to the user's needs.

To understand more, let's see an overview of the topics to be covered in this chapter:

- Publishing using publish utility
- Overview of Orchestration Server
- Using Orchestration Server to control bots
- Using Orchestration Server to deploy bots
- License management
- Publishing and managing updates

Publishing using publish utility

We design a workflow for some functionality so that it reduces our effort and time. When the workflow is successfully completed, we cannot afford to open UiPath time and again to run our workflow. So to use a workflow directly from the UiPath Robot, we have to publish our workflow first and then schedule it through Orchestrator. As soon as our workflow is published, we can directly run our workflow using a UiPath Robot from Orchestrator.

How to publish a workflow in UiPath

The following are the steps to be followed to publish a workflow in UiPath:

1. First, open UiPath Studio, create a new project, and give it an appropriate name.
2. Go to the **SETUP** Ribbon and click on the **Publish** button. Now check whether the project has been published successfully or not:

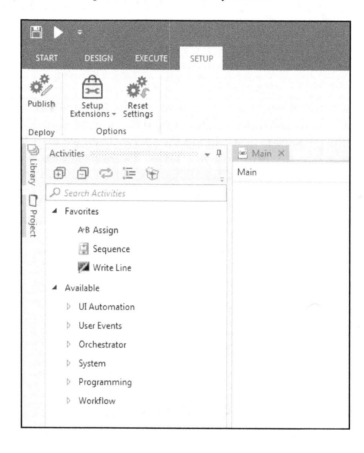

If the workflow has been published successfully, then a dialog box will appear containing all the necessary data required to run that workflow from Orchestrator:

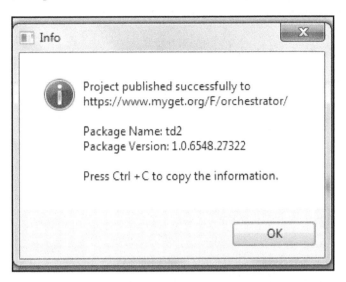

The **Info dialog** box displays all the information as mentioned in the following list:

1. The URL of the Orchestrator where the project is published.
2. The name of the package that has been published by you from UiPath Studio.
3. The version of the package that is published to Orchestrator. When we create any project in UiPath Studio then by default the path is saved in `C:\Users\username\Documents\UiPath` or it can be changed manually by the user. On creating a project, a folder is created that contains the following types of file:
    *   The `.screenshot` folder
    *   The `.xaml` file that is automatically created during automation
    *   `project.json`; this project file holds information about the project

When we publish the package to Orchestrator Server then it automatically reaches the server and can be viewed on the **Packages** page. However, if somehow the package is not found on the Orchestrator Server then we can add a package manually as well, as shown in the following steps:

1. Click on the **Upload Package** option:

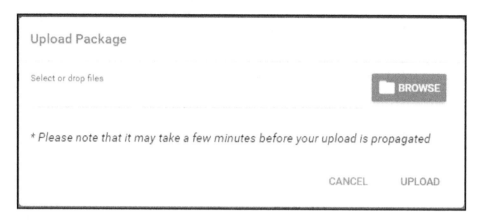

2. Click on **BROWSE** and navigate to the location to which your package was published in the first step.
3. Click on **UPLOAD**.
4. Now search for your package by clicking on **Processes** and then typing your package name in the empty Search box on the **Packages** page.

Writing/editing the published package info into the .json file

The .json file can be found inside the project. To edit the .json file in the project, we should follow the given steps:

1. Go to the project directory
2. Open the .json file in any editor, such as Notepad++
3. Now edit the main parameter of the automation project that you want to execute when the Orchestrator starts:

```
project - Notepad
File  Edit  Format  View  Help
{
    "name": "13",
    "description": "Blank Project",
    "main": "Main.xaml",
    "dependencies": {
        "UiPath.Core.Activities": "17.1.6522.14190"
    },
    "excludedData": [
        "Private:*",
        "*password*"
    ],
    "toolVersion": "17.1.6522.14204",
    "projectVersion": "1.0.6528.35408",
    "packOptions": {},
    "runtimeOptions": {}
}
```

4. Now save the .json file
5. Go to Orchestrator's **Processes** page and click on the **Packages** button

Overview of Orchestration Server

Using of Robots was not as popular as it is now. In other words, we can say that Robots worked within a limited environment. But today, due to **Robotic Process Automation (RPA)**, Robots can work in different environments. Nowadays, their performance is not limited. They are now playing a big role in terms of automation, working as assistant bots to fully potential Robots. They can work 24/7 and their operations can be managed and scheduled through the Orchestrator Server. UiPath Orchestrator is a web server that provides you with an environment for maintaining and scheduling your bots. Orchestrator is a highly accessible web server platform for fast deployment from one Robot to many Robots.

In autonomous automation techniques, one Robot can automate another Robot. This means a Robot can manage all the activities of another Robot-like process; scheduling, and so on.

Robots are of two types:

- Front office Robot (assistant Robot)
- Back office Robot

1. **Front office Robot (assistant Robot)**: Front office Robots act as a helping hand to its user. These are the Robots that require user interactions during the process. A Front office Robot is an agent assistant, which means the user is required to interact with the process. For example, the Robot requires the user to provide credentials or displays some message or dialog to which the user is required to respond otherwise further processes will not work. Some business processes are required to be performed by the trigger activity, in which once a task is triggered, the Robot is capable of running automation processes behind the lock screen.

2. **Back office Robot**: Back office Robots can log in to window sessions and run the automated process in unattended mode. They can be started with the help of Orchestrator. We can schedule these Robots or we can also run them manually using UiPath Robot or UiPath Studio.

UiPath Orchestrator has some logical components, which are given as follows:

1. User Interface Layer:
   - Web Application

2. Web Services Layer:
   - Monitoring Service
   - Logging Service
   - Deployment Service
   - Configuration Service
   - Queues Service

3. Persistence Layer:
   - SQL Server
   - ElasticSearch

Queues

Queues work as a container that stores tasks that need to be implemented. Simply imagine a group of boys standing in a queue in front of a ticketing counter. The logic is that the person who goes in first gets out first. **First In First Out (FIFO)**.

Similarly, in the case of Robots, when we have a number of operations that are to be performed and when the server is busy, then tasks are moved in a queue and they are implemented on the same logic **First In First Out (FIFO)**.

To create a new queues, search for the Queue option in the Orchestrator Server listed on the left-hand side and then inside the Queue page, you can add one. It also allows you to access all those **Queues** that have already been created. It contains some information about the task such as the remaining time, progress time, average time, description, and so on, as listed in the following screenshot:

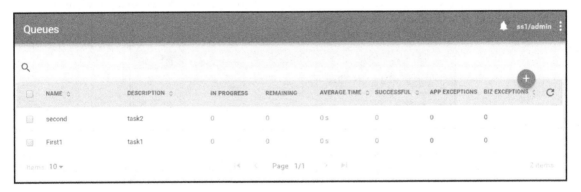

We can also add queue items from UiPath Studio and there are various activities that support this feature, which are listed as follows:

- **Add Queue Item**: This activity is used to add a new item to the queue in Orchestrator. The status of the item will be New.
- **Add Transaction Item**: This activity is used to add an item to the queue to begin transaction and set the status as In Progress. Here we can add custom reference for each respective transaction.
- **Get Transaction Item**: This activity is used to get an item from the queue to process it and set its status as In Progress.

- **Postpone Transaction Item**: This activity is used to define time parameters between which transaction should be processed. Here, basically, we will specify the time interval after which a process will start.
- **Set Transaction Progress**: Used to assist and create custom progress statuses for In Progress transactions. To notify its progress if the process crashes. This activity plays a significant role in tackling troubleshooting processes.
- **Set Transaction Status**: Used to modify the status of the transaction item; whether it fails or is successful.

Assets

Assets work as variables or credentials and can be used in distinct automation projects. Assets provides the opportunity to hold specific information. This information can be easily accessed by the Robot. The Assets activity can be found from the **Activities** panel, as given in the following screenshot:

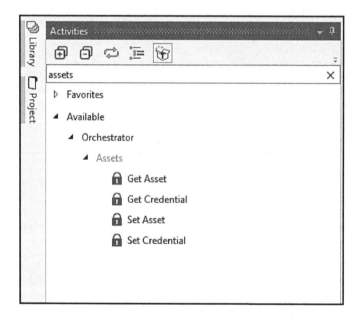

In addition, assets can also be used for security purposes to store credentials. As we know, all credentials are stored in encrypted format by the AES 256 algorithm. When an RPA developer is designing a process, it can be invoked by the developer, but its value is still hidden.

To create a new asset in Orchestrator, we are required to open the **Assets** page. It also shows all the previously created assets that can be removed or edited:

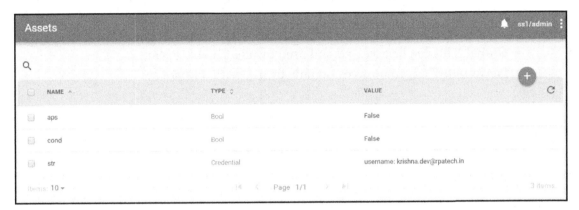

Assets are of two types:

1. Get Asset
2. Get Credential

The **Get Asset** and **Get Credential** activities are used in Studio to request information from Orchestrator about a specific asset, according to a provided `AssetName`.

The `AssetName` is required for an already stored asset in the Orchestrator database so that the Robot can access the information stored in Asset. To do so, the Robot needs permission to retrieve information from that particular asset to be used in the automation project. We can get assets using the **Get Asset** activity in the **Activities** panel of UiPath Studio as explained earlier.

There are four types of asset values:

1. **Text**: This holds string values.
2. **Boolean**: This supports only true or false values.
3. **Integer**: This stores integer values.
4. **Credential**: This holds usernames and passwords that are needed by the Robot to execute specific processes, such as login details.

Furthermore, we also have the following types of Asset:

- **Global**: This can be accessed and used by all available Robots
- **Per Robot**: This can be accessed only by a specified Robot

Process

The process is responsible for deploying and uploading the package to the Orchestrator environment, and for deploying already created packages. In UiPath Studio, we can search for Process inside the **Orchestrator** option available in the **Activities** panel. It contains a **Should Stop** activity that can be used to stop a process whenever required:

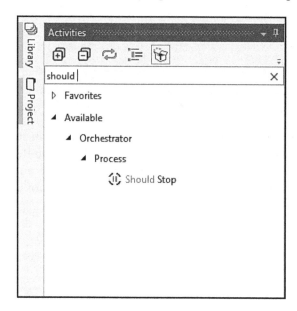

Processes assist in distributing all **Packages** over the Robot machine, which makes execution faster. We can assign jobs to these processes from the jobs panel available in the left corner in Orchestrator:

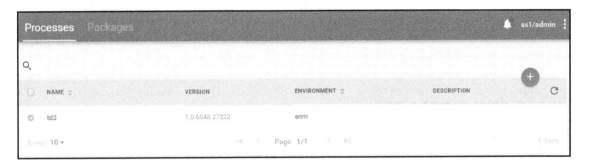

At every stage a package is linked to the environment and it is automatically distributed with each Robot machine that belongs to a particular environment. Whenever you make changes in the package you created earlier and upload those changes, it creates a new version of that package. Thus, in order to update your package, you can go to the **Manage versions** option available on that package and select the version of that package that you want to use:

If a new update to a certain package is available then an icon is displayed on that package.

When we are using the latest available version of a package with a specific process, then the icon will show next to the process. All activities that we are using in Studio are stored in the NuGet feed that Orchestrator has access to. While we add a new process, the name of the environment should be the same as that of the Robot. This allows the execution of processes using respective Robots.

Deploying a process

Deploying a process basically refers to the distribution of the packages to the Robots available.

After successfully publishing your project from UiPath Studio, as explained earlier, we can follow these following steps to deploy a process:

1. Open the Orchestrator web page.
2. Click the **Processes** option on the left side.
3. **Processes** windows will appear on the web page.
4. Now click the **+** button to add a package. The **Deploy Process** windows will be displayed.
5. Now choose the desired package name from the drop-down list (package here corresponds to the project you have published from UiPath Studio).

6. Here, the description option is optional.

7. Finally, click the **CREATE** button to deploy the process:

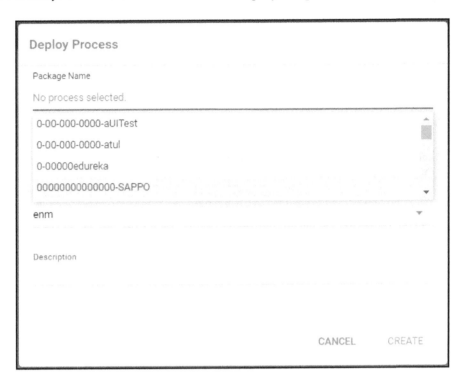

Using Orchestration Server to control bots

When it comes to controlling a Robot Orchestrator is the best option. Orchestration Server can be used to schedule bots so that Robots can execute their jobs within the time interval specified on the server. Orchestrator can control an unlimited number of Robots and we can very easily assign various tasks to the Robots as per the user's needs. Also, a specific task can be assigned to multiple Robots. Orchestrator also gives us the facility to maintain all logs generated by the Robot.

Robot statuses

The status of a Robot tells us about its availability and connectivity. We get to know whether the Robot is available, busy, or disconnected. The following are the statuses that a Robot can have:

- **Available**: This status of the Robot shows that the Robot is not working on any other task and is freely available to take tasks
- **Busy**: This type of status will be shown when a Robot is currently executing some task and is not available
- **Disconnected**: This status of Robot shows that your Robot is no longer connected to Orchestrator Server

Editing the Robot

Sometimes we may have to edit the Robot in Orchestrator in case the Robot is either not functioning properly or we want to assign some other tasks to the Robot.

To edit the Robot, click on the Edit button from the Edit window and change the name or the necessary fields as given:

- Name
- Username
- Password
- Type
- Description:

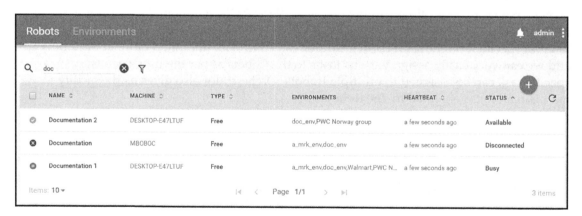

Deleting the Robot

When a Robot is not working at all, it is necessary to remove it, and we can use either of the following:

- To delete the desired Robot, select that Robot and go to the admin screen by clicking on the Admin tag on the top of the Orchestrator Server window. Then select the **More Action** button and delete the Robot.

- If you want to delete one or more Robots from the page, we can select them or remove them from the page.

Displaying logs for a Robot

To view logs of a Robot, go to the Robots page and search for your desired Robot, click on **More Actions**, and then click on **View logs** to view log messages from your Robot:

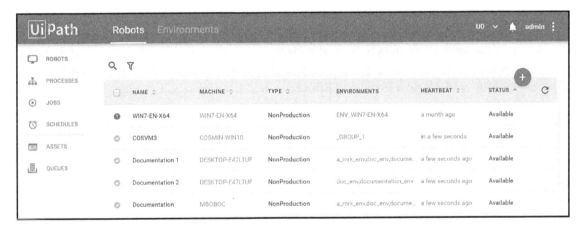

Using Orchestration Server to deploy bots

To deploy Robots to Orchestrator, we need to configure the machine with Orchestrator. To do this, we first have to create a provisioning Robot from the Orchestrator URL: `http://platform.uipath.com`.

Creating a provision Robot from the Orchestrator

The user needs; permissions to register the new Robot and they must have the following information:

- The name of the machine and the key required to connect to Orchestrator. They can be found through the **Control Panel** | **System**, for the key, log on to the Orchestrator URL, click on the **ROBOTS** page, then click on the + button. A pop up window appears where your key is visible. **Security** | **System** and **User** | **Settings** | **Deployment**, which provides us the Robot API Key.
- The username and password of the specified machine to access it.
- To create the provision Robot, go to the Orchestrator. Click on the Robot option on the left side of the Orchestrator page.
- After displaying the Robot page, click on the + button. It will display a small window to create a provision Robot:

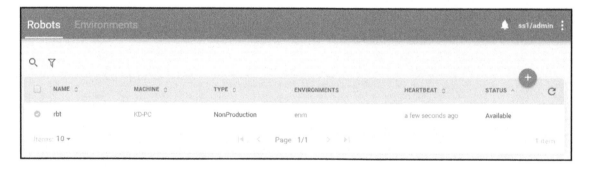

- After the window is displayed, fill in all the mandatory information that is required to connect the Robot—machine name, Robot name, username/domain name, password, type, and description, as given in the following screenshot:

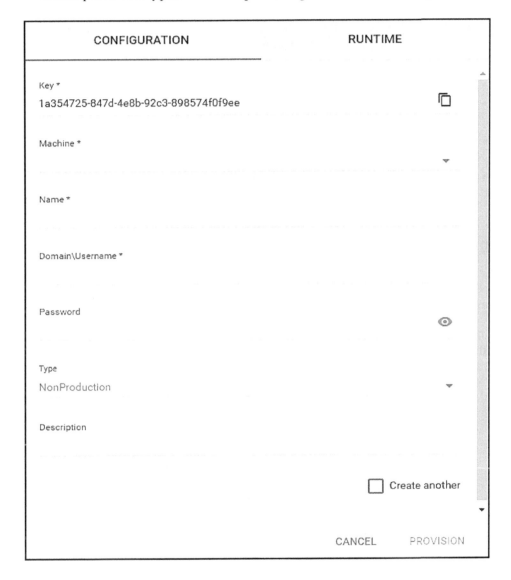

- In the **Machine** * field section, enter the **machine** name that is required to connect to Orchestrator.
- From the **Name** * field enter the desired name of the Robot.
- Now in the **Domain\Username** * field, type the name that will be used to log in to the defined machine. Here, we need to define the format **Domain/Username** * if the user is in the domain. It is compulsory to choose a short domain name.
- **Password** field is optional; it can be skipped.
- We can choose the type of Robot from the drop-down list.
- **The description** field is also optional. You can give a short summary describing your Robot.
- Now copy the Robot **Key** * and paste the key in UiPath Robot while configuring your Robot.
- Click the **PROVISION** button and the Robot will be displayed on the Robot page.

Connecting a Robot to Orchestrator

When we deploy a Robot to Orchestrator, we must have the machine name and the key for each Robot. To keep the value of these fields, we can create another Robot from the **Provisional Robot** windows.

If we want to create a new Robot, we have to take authentication from administrator. By default, the administrator has the right to register a new Robot.

To connect the Robot machine to Orchestrator, follow the given steps:

1. From the system taskbar, click on UiPath Robot. The **Robots** windows will be displayed:

2. Now go to **Options** and choose **Settings...**; the Robot Settings will be displayed:

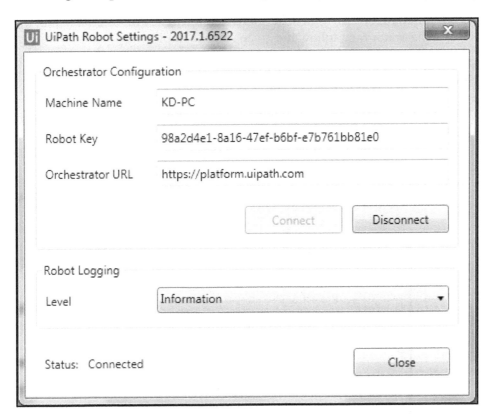

3. In the **Robot Key** field, paste the received key of provision Robot to Orchestrator.
4. In the **Orchestrator URL** field, enter the address of the Orchestrator.
5. Now click the **Connect** button. After clicking the **Connect** button, the Robot will connect to the Orchestrator.

Deploy the Robot to Orchestrator

To deploy our Robot, first of all, it must be connected to Orchestrator. Ensure that our bot is connected to Orchestrator then follow the given steps to deploy it:

1. First of all, install UiPath on the machine.
2. Provision the Robot machine and take the Robot key from Orchestrator.
3. After receiving the key go to the Robot configuration panel and enter the key here.
4. Also, you need to enter the Robot key into the configuration URL, which can be found from the admin section of Orchestrator.
5. Publish the project with publish utility from UiPath. When it is published successfully, it will display the information shown in the following screenshot:

6. The project has been published in the Orchestrator.

7. To create the environment, go to the home page, click on the **ROBOTS** option, and click on the **Environments** Tab. Then click on the **+** button:

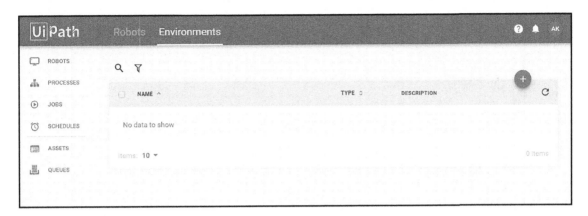

8. Once the details are filled in, click on **Create**:

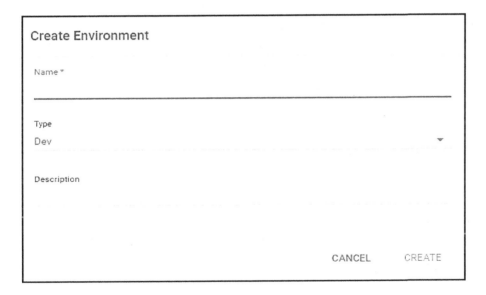

9. After creating the environment, a small window will appear as shown in the following screenshot, where we can manage the Robot within the environment:

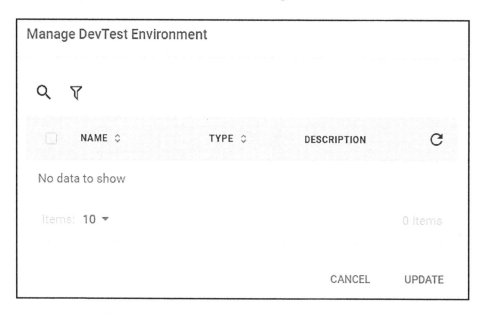

10. After clicking on the + button, a will window pop-up where we can choose the Published package, as shown in the following screenshot, and then click on the **CREATE** button:

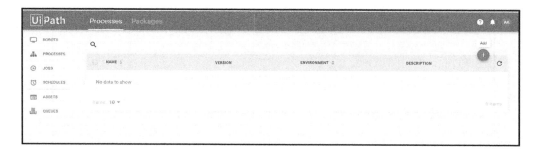

11. After clicking the **Deploy Process** button, a window popup will appear where we can choose the published package, as shown in the following screenshot, and then click on the **CREATE** button.

Or

12. Packages can be manually uploaded from the local directory after clicking the **View Packages** option and then clicking the **Upload** button as given in the following screenshot: **PROCESS** | **View Packages** | **Upload Packages**:

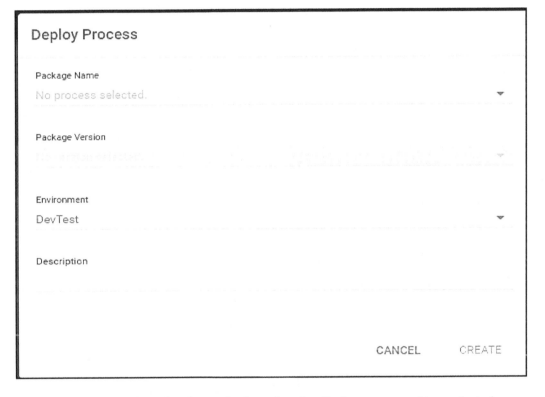

13. Now the package has been deployed to the Orchestrator and is ready to be executed through the web.
14. Next, click the **JOBS** option for execution and click on the **Start** icon as shown:

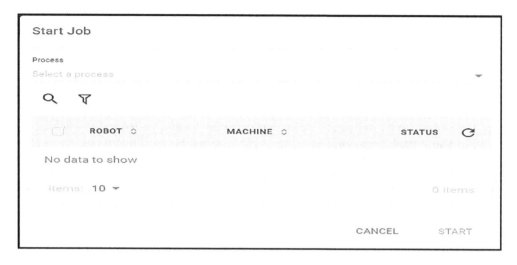

15. After clicking the **Start Job** button, the Robot will execute over Orchestrator.

License management

To manage and deploy bots, we are required to register the license on their server. Once you have received the license, the deployment and maintenance processes become faster.

Activating and uploading a license to Orchestrator

After getting the license code from the sales support team or any centralized location, we need to follow the given steps to activate the license and upload it to Orchestrator:

1. It is mandatory to have the UiPath Platform installed on the local machine.
2. If the UiPath Platform is not available then install it.
3. Now open the Command Prompt as an administrator account from the local machine.

4. Here we can change the directory for installing the path manually with the command `cd C:\Program Files (x86)\UiPath Platform\UiPath`.

5. To activate a license, we need the Regutil tool. If this tool is available, then type the following command to activate it through the command line: `regutil activate /email=emailaddress /code=licensecode`.

6. Now export the license information to the file using the command `regutil export-info /out_file=D:\license.txt`.

7. Go to Orchestrator and click the **Admin** option. Then select the **Settings** page from the drop-down list:

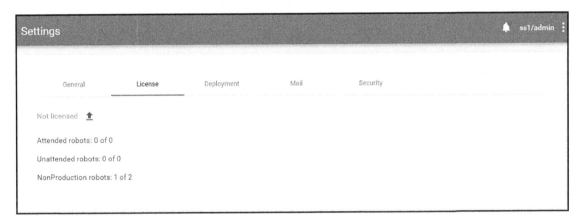

8. As the **Settings** page becomes visible, we can see the **License** tab, as shown in the preceding screenshot. Click on **License**. Then under the **License** portion of the page, we can see our available license with an option for uploading it. Click on the **Upload** option.

After successfully uploading the license, navigate to the license information, which is created by using the Regutil tool and the uploading methodology. Here, the license expiry date of each Robot can be checked. Whenever we connect a new Robot to Orchestrator, it consumes a new license.

Publishing and managing updates

When we successfully create a workflow that can be used to perform certain automation, it should be published. This is necessary because, if we open UiPath Studio and run the workflow each time we require it, then it will consume a lot of time and also require human involvement to do it. This is not the right approach while automating. Hence, we publish our workflow so that it can run very easily using UiPath Robot or Orchestrator. Sometimes, we may want to make some changes to the workflow that we published earlier. For that, we have to make changes and publish it again so that the latest workflow is available on Orchestrator. This workflow is also updated to the latest version.

 In this section, we will understand how to publish a project and how to update it.

Packages

When projects are published to Orchestrator from UiPath Studio, they become packages. These packages can be found on the **Process** page after clicking on the **Packages** option.

Published packages are shown in the following screenshot:

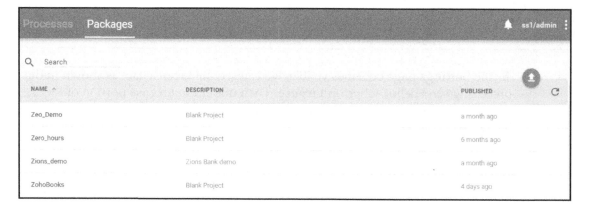

Orchestrator provides the facility to update, view, or delete your packages from the **Packages** page. Every package in Orchestrator contains a version, its published date, and its description. Suppose we have a package and we want to make changes to that package, say, we have added some new functionality to that package from UiPath Studio and publish it again. In order to use the newest version of that uploaded package, we can view that package from the **Packages** page, as shown in the preceding screenshot, and then it will display all the available package versions for that package. In order to update the version, either select the version of your choice or click on **Get the latest version** to use the latest uploaded version of that package:

Manage versions for td2_enm

LATEST   ROLLBACK

VERSION	PUBLISHED	USED	C
1.0.6549.23598	3 hours ago		
1.0.6549.23513	3 hours ago		
1.0.6548.27322 Current	a day ago	a day ago	

Items: 10 ▼ |◄ <   Page 1/1   > ►| 3 items

CANCEL

In the preceding screenshot, the user can view and delete all published packages that were published to Orchestrator.

Package versions can have two statuses:

- **Active**: When a package version is in active mode then it means that the version is currently in use
- **Inactive**: If a package version is inactive then it means that this version is not in use

Managing packages

After a package has been created on the Orchestrator Server, we can easily view them in the **Packages** tab on the **Processes** page. Here, we can upload or remove packages.

Uploading packages

When we publish our project to the Orchestration server, it will automatically send the package to the server. If we want, we can upload the package manually as well. For that, Orchestrator provides the facility to upload a project manually from the local machine. To upload packages, we need to follow the given steps:

1. Navigate to the **Processes** page, select the **Packages** option, and then click on Upload packages. A dialog will appear in the window like in the following screenshot:

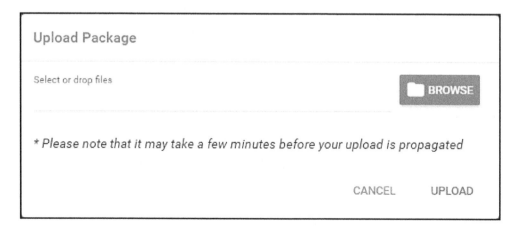

2. Now click the **BROWSE** button and select the packages from the local machine with a name for the uploaded file.

3. After selecting the proper package click on the **UPLOAD** button so that the package becomes available with the currently existing packages on the **Packages** page.

Deleting packages

When we no longer require a package then we can easily delete it. Make sure that the process is not in active mode. We can just select our package and click on the **Remove** button. We may also remove multiple packages at the same time by checking one or more packages from the list or by clicking on the **REMOVE ALL INACTIVE** tab to remove all packages that are inactive:

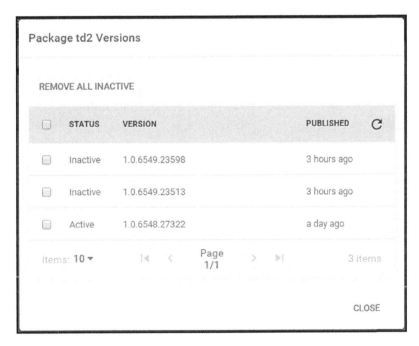

Summary

As we approach towards the end of the book, let us quickly go through what we learnt. We started off by learning about RPA, its scope, and some tools available for RPA. Then we delved into more details about UiPath, its components, and setting up UiPath Studio to train your own bot. You also got to know about the user interface for UiPath Studio before beginning to design your first Robot. Once comfortable enough, we explored a fascinating aspect of UiPath, that is, recording. In Chapter 3, *Sequence, Flowchart, and Control Flow*, we saw how a workflow was structured and the different types of project available in UiPath—when they are used and how to use them. Chapter 3, *Sequence, Flowchart, and Control Flow*, also introduced you to activities and how to manually drag and drop activities to make our workflow, all this in the user-friendly interface provided by UiPath Studio!

In Chapters 4 through 7, we went deeper into UiPath: we learned more about recording, about data manipulation, the various controls in UiPath, about extraction, selectors, OCR data scraping, and screen scraping. We also read about the various plugins available and about assistant bots.

That's not all; an important aspect of your automation journey is properly organizing your project, as well as being prepared for handling exceptions. All of these were dealt with in detail in Chapter 8, *Exception Handling, Debugging, and Logging*, and Chapter 9, *Managing and Maintaining the Code*.

Finally, you were taught how to deploy your bot.

From being a novice at the beginning of the book, you are now skilled enough to develop and deploy a bot! Your automation journey has begun!

Other Books You May Enjoy

If you enjoyed this book, you may be interested in these other books by Packt:

Learning ServiceNow
Tim Woodruff

ISBN: 978-1-78588-332-3

- Acquire and configure your own free personal developer instance of ServiceNow
- Read (and write!) clear, effective requirements for ServiceNow development
- Avoid common pitfalls and missteps that could seriously impact future progress and upgradeability
- Know how to troubleshoot when things go wrong using debugging tools
- Discover developer "tips and tricks"
- Pick up great tips from top ServiceNow development and administration professionals, and find out what they wish they knew when they were starting out

ServiceNow Automation
Ashish Rudra Srivastava

ISBN: 978-1-78588-576-1

- Understand the Importance and the power of automation.
- Replace unstructured work patterns with intelligent workflows.
- Identify the components of the ServiceNow user interface.
- Learn to automate and align business service workflows across the organization in support of the core mission.
- Perform an objective-based analysis that delivers a business case presenting the costs and benefits associated with migrating from legacy solutions to ServiceNow

Leave a review - let other readers know what you think

Please share your thoughts on this book with others by leaving a review on the site that you bought it from. If you purchased the book from Amazon, please leave us an honest review on this book's Amazon page. This is vital so that other potential readers can see and use your unbiased opinion to make purchasing decisions, we can understand what our customers think about our products, and our authors can see your feedback on the title that they have worked with Packt to create. It will only take a few minutes of your time, but is valuable to other potential customers, our authors, and Packt. Thank you!

Index

Made in United States
North Haven, CT
02 March 2022

16716403R10200